Gallery Books
Editor: Peter Fallon

ALL SOULS

Michael Coady

ALL SOULS

Gallery Books

All Souls
is first published
simultaneously in paperback
and in a clothbound edition
on 12 December 1997.

The Gallery Press
Loughcrew
Oldcastle
County Meath
Ireland

ISBN 1 85235 211 6 (*paperback*)
    1 85235 212 4 (*clothbound*)

The Gallery Press acknowledges the financial assistance
of An Chomhairle Ealaíon / The Arts Council, Ireland,
and the Arts Council of Northern Ireland.

Contents

for Martina,
Niamh, Lucy and James

If there's no hatred in a mind
Assault and battery of the wind
Can never tear the linnet from the leaf.
— W. B. Yeats

VOICES

The Blind Arch

I always loved it on a morning like this, the way the rising sun touches the slope above the river first of all. Then the way it floods down over the roofs and through the eight arches of the old stone bridge, except for the blind arch under the quay where the stream turns into the dark and then out below at an angle. Not that it matters at all now whether the sun is shining or the tide coming or going. Or whether wind is whining through the arches or there's November mist in the laneways or hard frost over the town clock or torrents of rain down Bridge Street in the small hours with not a sinner out. Still, there's something about morning sun that goes straight to the heart of things.

Here comes your man now on the bike, round the bend at the top of the hill, past the milkman who's surprised to see him out this early, and down to the bridge where Sam Ryan is already out casting a line for salmon, with Ellen gone off for the day with a busload of the Third Order of St Francis on a mystery tour ending with the vigil at the moving statue outside Cappoquin. And there's the town clock bell that's sounding since Mozart was alive in the world, though you'd never know when to believe the story it tells.

In any case here he is again today with the pen and the big red notebook to take down all the particulars — repose of the soul of, in loving memory, and all the rest of it. Repose of the soul. How easy it is once you're through and out on the other side. Alfie, I said to him the first time he took me out on the river, Alfie, I said, take me back to dry land before you put the heart crossways in me. And he swung the cot in under the weir and shot her in under the blind arch of the bridge where it was pitch dark until he sank the paddle into the tide to turn her sideways and then all of a sudden we were through the tunnel and out on the stream below with the light dazzling our eyes.

Seen from where the others are looking, this slope that the morning sun touches first is a place of tears. Parting with children was worst of all, even if I had none of my own. The little white box going into a hole in the ground. Enough to break the heart inside of you and leave you demented. Enough to make you want to throw yourself into the tide. And the girls and young men that coughed their way here with consumption. My own brother

13

Martin only nineteen with the cold sweat on him and my mother beside herself holding him in her arms as he was going. Oh Jesus, there's enough pain and misery in the world to earn us all heaven twice over and no questions asked.

Well there's no fear of us here, beyond all wind and weather. On our way to some kind of salvation. Adrift in this dream while we wait for the last great call and, Mother of God, that will be the day and no mistake. The big finale with the entire company brought back on the stage. In our own shapes, mind you, or so we used to believe before they did away with the Latin. *Et exspecto resurrectionem mortuorum*. Because we wouldn't be our own true selves without the four bones we were born with. In the twinkling of an eye. At the last trumpet. Some music it will take to gather up all the pieces and put them together again. Professor Gebler at the organ in Waterford Cathedral when I was a student. *Never fear mistakes when you play! Great music means that there is nothing to fear. Surrender yourself to the music. It tells us that the soul must never be afraid.*

They pass through here regularly, the ones that are still above ground. Taking the handy shortcut from Friary Height to Abbey Square. Going for milk or rashers or the morning paper. Some that would talk the teeth out of a saw. *You remember him, he had a shop at the top of Oven Lane, that was married to Kitty Banks, she used to make lovely bread.*

Some that would argue the toss with Christ and his blessèd mother. And some not sober coming back from their morning errands. Charlie Cleary talking to himself as he shuffles in the gate, tripping over gravestones in broad daylight. Sitting down to get his bearings on top of Theobald O'Donnell, Esq. and his belovèd wife, Hanora. Singing *Oh if I had the wings of a swallow* as soon as he gets his wind, *I would travel far over the sea* as he empties his bladder behind a Celtic cross carved by hand before the Boer War. Rows and arguments they carry in here as well. Whether he should go down on top of his wife or his mother. Who went where before, and who comes next in order. Sacred Heart, the things that bother them. And all of us easy in one bed where there's room for all comers and one as good as the next, with flowers springing up over the lot of us though you might call them weeds if you cared to be particular.

So look at your man now, doing the rounds of this place with poppies standing up red between the grey stones and crosses. No end of insects working away in the grass and weeds, the birds singing, and all the particulars going down from stone on to paper. The sun climbing over the hill and the tide flooding up to the weir below. My own house down there too with the windows bricked up nowadays and a young sycamore growing out of the chimney.

Maybe he's learning something from the census he's taking, though there's lots not written on stone. I could tell him the lovely man that his grandfather was and a good musician considering that he taught himself anything he knew. A bit of a chancer too, though I never told anyone that, did I? On the narrow stairs down from the organ loft after Midnight Mass on Christmas Eve, with the two of us married already. Some drink on his breath of course and I gave him a piece of my mind. Trying to kiss me inside in the church and no shame on him. What women know about men could break windows all over the town. He's down there below now with Minnie that held out twenty years after him in spite of her bad hip. And her people that thought him a fool for playing the fiddle instead of minding the shop. Not much talk out of them now with all the bad debts gone away with the tide.

I suppose if I knew him before Alfie I might have married him, with the music such a great draw between us. We had an understanding anyway with nothing ever said. He'd always wait on when I played a piece after Mass even though it meant they'd be last out from the church. Minnie, by the way, listening beside him that wouldn't know Bach from Three Blind Mice. Closer than that we never got apart from that kiss on Christmas Eve.

Anyway it was all decided before that between Alfie and myself. My freshwater sailor from Passage East. *I'm a qualified marine engineer that sailed the three sister rivers since I was a boy.* Ructions raised by his people and my own as well because he was a Protestant. But we bested them all except for the fact that we had neither chick nor child and some of them thought it a judgement.

I'm a freshwater sailor washed up on the tide, he said the very first time I met him at the Regatta dance when he asked me to play the piano for his party piece. A small enough man, but a voice as deep as a cave. I felt some kind of shock down to my toes when I heard him that night filling up the boathouse and silencing everyone there. *And when Sergeant Death in his cold arms shall take me, Oh lull me to sleep with your Erin go bragh*. Then letting on that he wanted lessons in reading music and voice training so that he could come calling.

Oh yes they had a mind to block us but we bested them all and had our own time and our sweetness. One night I'll never forget when we were newly married I went down by boat on the quiet with him as far as Waterford, though he could lose his job as skipper if Mr Malcolmson ever found out. A tartan rug wrapped around me sitting beside him at the wheel, with a brandy flask between us and sweet-cake. The moon shining and the tide in the Long Reach so still and perfect that you'd swear you could walk across it like Our Lord.

How innocent the river looks. Like a cat in the lap of the land. But the wildness there just under the skin. That night in December below Portnaboe, Joe Dwyer making tea in the galley when he felt her swinging out of control and up on a mud-bank. Running up to find Alfie gone over the side and beyond his reach in the dark. With myself at home in bed asleep and innocent not knowing that Malcolmson would be at my door in his stiff collar at seven in the morning. And no sign of him then or ever after though they dragged for weeks in the worst of the winter all the way down the estuary.

The rest of it was nights and days and whiskey and not caring what I did or who saw me. If only they found him I could have worked my way through it in time. If only they found him I could have grieved like many another and made up some face for the world. If only they brought some part of him home to me. The Christmas Eve I fell face down at the organ and Fr Benignus told me I'd have to resign. The night of spilling rain that the sergeant picked me up on the bridge in my night-dress.

After that the locks and corridors, the lights and pills and faces. Was it weeks or years I was there?

How easy it is in the end once you let go. Though he's not with me here I know that all is well. All is well though everything slips from our grasp. Though everything breaks and crumbles.

Here on this slope your man is fishing for names and dates that are told on stone. Maybe he'll learn it's not about things fixed on stone at all, but about a river of moments where everything filters down to the bed and nothing at all is lost. On the bridge Sam Ryan flexes the greenheart rod in the sunshine and sends a long cast looping over the pool below the weir, hoping to have a salmon laid out in the scullery when Ellen gets home tonight from her mystery tour.

Loaves and Fishes

from the telling of a Carrick cot-fisherman

I remember two blank weeks
we fished in the month of February —
nights so bitter my father
had to hoist me stiff from the cot
before we'd limp home in the frost.

In the third week we caught a big salmon
like a gift from God, at Tinhalla.
He near broke the net — a pure
bar of silver and fit for a king
fresh up from the sea on the tide.

Salmon were for sale, not for eating.
In the morning we landed the fish
on the steps of Gregg Hall, while the maid
went to consult with the master
as soon as he'd finish his breakfast.

Two pounds was what we were asking,
with six of us waiting for bread.
In a while she came back with a shilling:
he would take a piece of the salmon,
but it had to be centre cut.

I hope he's not hungry or cold
stretched in his vault now in Whitechurch.
My father brought home the full fish.
He divided it out with the neighbours
and we fed for a day like the gentry.

Full Forward

He used to pull up his shirt in pubs
to show off the hole in his side
he got from the dig of a hurley in Muckalee —

whenever he captured the ball
both umpires automatically
reached for their flags.

In latter years
he used to stoke
the furnace in the Mental;

he lit up a statue
to Our Lady
in his garden

and played the bodhrán
for wild nights
in the Jug of Punch.

They buried him in Lamogue
but the sons came back from England
and ruz him up again years after

to plant him in Aghavillar.

A Soldier's Parable

In Templemore
during the Emergency
the barracks was walking
alive with rats

and all the cures
in the wide
earthly world
had been tried.

In the end we trapped
a few dozen alive
and left them
to starve in a cage

until they began
to tear
and eat
each other.

At last there was only
the one left alive
and he was a king
and a cannibal.

So we set him loose
and in less than a month
he had cleared the place
of his kind —

except that the men
couldn't shut an eye
until a crack shot
was sent up from Fermoy.

Awakening

Sister Imelda rising
on the last day —

words she could have
sworn she heard
the bishop speak

before she awakes
high in the organ loft
of another evening

blinks through her glasses
and complains
in her old self

that the girls
are late again
for evening devotions.

Alone in her habit
she settles to sing
Bring flowers of the fairest

until it dawns on her
that someone has pulled out
all the stops

and the light
is coming
from another angle.

She should have
been told about
these changes

with the girls as usual
dallying on their way
to clatter up the stairs

and pant excuses
in the middle of
the Divine Praises.

Sister Imelda rising
on the last day
misses her arthritis:

she lifts her head
to read a music
without lines and spaces.

VISITATIONS

Time's Kiss

SERVANT GIRL

All that remains
is the ruin among trees
and a name
in an old man's mouth —

*They say he took off in the end
with a servant girl
by the name of
Lucy Honey.*

OLD WOMAN

The past is a wind
that moans behind her,
a draught around a door
she can't keep closed.

The Public Record

Outside there are clouds
and cars and shoppers,
men placing bets. In here

you could become obsessed
as a man replaying fall of dice
or cards turned over —

the illiterate boatman you uncover
in your blood, the shock of your
great-grandmother's excited girl's

hand in the marriage register,
lost children that she bore
snuffed out like little candles

by meningitis, measles or pneumonia
where now you know
a supermarket carpark.

You begin to feel
a kind of terror
at the weight

of what lies stacked
from floor to ceiling
all about you

while the girl
who keeps things
up to date

and in their proper order
is laughing on the phone
about what dress she'll wear

for the wedding
that she's going to
next Saturday.

The Cross

Three of you barred
at the cross above Bridge Street
with pain of Good Friday
red-raw in your eyes,

each of you looking
for cure or forgiveness
to streets that are shuttered
and wells that are dry.

Today there's no stranger
to touch as he passes,
no word that might salve
the pain of your loss —

you sweat out the vigil
while burgher and publican
are up in the chapel
kissing the cross.

The Well of Cuan

Oisín and Patrick
still contend
upon this ground.

At fall of night on Pattern Day
country music throbs
from Kiely's public house

to infiltrate
the shadowed fields
outside the window

of the priest
who whispers night
prayers to the Virgin.

He unhooks his collar,
sees the cat out,
bolts the door

and goes to bed.

Watching 'The Dead' in the Living Room

We are all
becoming shades
but these revellers
who've crashed in
don't want to see
what's showing
on this last night
of the year.

I sulk within my corner
watching Huston's ghost retell
each cadence of the story
until I think I see
its blind begetter rise
and slip across the room

      to focus on the blessèd
      myopia of the living
      and join the opposition
      of drink and cards and laughter

      as if to say that there,
      not here,
      is all the party,
      all the story.

The Picture House

Under one roof for fifty years
our town divided into three;
balcony, parterre and pit defined
the truth of caste in our community.

In the democracy of dark
from plush above to piss below
we drank in with avid eyes
a common wine of fantasy

until red helmets and blue denim
of Phoenix Demolition
rode in to town one day
to let in light and air

and bring down
all the terraced
protocol of years.

The Club

You don't realise until you're forty or so
that by then everyone of your age or more
is walking around with some old wound that's buried
back of the eyes or somewhere under the coat.

Even then you forget that some of those you pass
with a nod every day on the road took their hits
quite early on, though you may not remember ever
seeing them stumble or fall or hearing them moan

since that was before the water cleared to show
that wounding seems part of some general plan, with rules
that are not just bloody unfair, they're bloody unknown.
Strange how it took so long for the light to dawn

that sooner or later your own due turn would come
to take one in the shoulder or the gut,
entitling you to limp into the club,
a member in good standing, now fully paid-up.

Trumpet Player

Sidemen he once led
have made it just in time
to lip cold brass and chance

an unrehearsed *Abide With Me*
between the last Amen
and sluice of clay.

His silence underscores
fluffed notes
and broken phrases,

compels
reunion and farewell
for all their nights

of mud and alchemy
on tented greens
of little towns —

golden blaze of trumpet
quickening the canvas
and the crowd

heroicizing
carnal risk
and glitter in the ring.

Now more than ever
must they envy him
his brazen sorcery:

was it in his breath-control
or lucky shape
of mouth?

Adagio Cantabile

for Pierre Reach, pianist; Kilkenny, 1995

When hands touched chords
and Beethoven entered
the cathedral

the infant
might have cried
but did not,

the mother lifting him
from lap to breast
with utter confidence

in a music
learned by heart
and played by ear

like long
and wordless looks
between rapt lovers,

like song replete
with tenderness
as candlelight in corners

and easeful
space within
the touched vibrations

for counterpointed
sighings of content
and primal murmurings

gracing ancient air
and stone with
an intimate authority

in which the space,
the music and the child
compelled communion

so that mute centuries
of dead were eased
and recomposed

from beds
of stone again
into warm cradles

and breathed with
the living
in a mystery

where every gathered
soul again became
an infant at the breast

in a cathedral
cradled round
a font in which

the fish of time
swims in the ocean
of eternity.

Outside the windows
enfolding dark
composed a nocturne

like a blessing
on a harvest
safely home.

THREE MEN STANDING
AT THE MET

LA FORZA DEL DESTINO

(THE FORCE OF DESTINY)

OPERA IN FOUR ACTS (EIGHT SCENES)
(IN ITALIAN)
BOOK BY FRANCESCO MARIA PIAVE

MUSIC by GIUSEPPE VERDI

MARQUIS OF CALATRAVA	LOUIS D'ANGELO
DONNA LEONORA	ROSA PONSELLE
DON CARLOS OF VARGAS	MARIO BASIOLA
DON ALVARO	GIOVANNI MARTINELLI
PREZIOSILLA	INA BOURSKAYA
THE ABBOT	EZIO PINZA
FATHER MELITONE	POMPILIO MALATESTA
CURRA	PHILINE FALCO (*debut*)
THE ALCADE	PAOLO ANANIAN
TRABUCO	GIORDANO PALTRINIERI
A SURGEON	VINCENZO RESCHIGLIAN

Incidental Dances by CORPS DE BALLET

CONDUCTOR	VINCENZO BELLEZZA

STAGE DIRECTOR	SAMUEL THEWMAN
CHORUS MASTER	GIULIO SETTI
STAGE MANAGER	ARMANDO AGNINI

Positively No Encores Allowed

New York City. Friday, November 4, 1927. That was then and this is now. Or maybe vice versa. Now is Saturday, March 16, 1996, and I'm tuning to a live broadcast of Verdi's *La Forza del Destino* from the Metropolitan Opera House. The music soars out of New York City to a satellite in space, overleaps an ocean, finds my study in a small town in an Irish river valley, animates the air between my bookshelves, earthing through my uncle Peter's battered old trombone which hangs in the corner. All in a micro-second of transmission time from there to here. What has this to do with poetry? With some cosmic harmony of hearts? With the music of what happens?

There are conspiring shades about me, standing again, listening to *La Forza del Destino* as they did on that November evening at the 'Old' Met in 1927. I have — spread before me as I listen — the printed programme which my future father sent back to impress his own father in Ireland. His written words upon the page which

shows the seating plan: *This is where we stood.* His X which
marks the place. *It is a passageway leading to the Orchestra seats.*

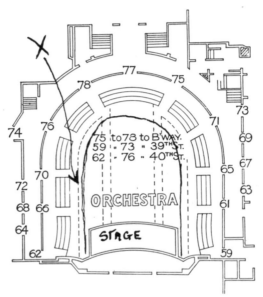

this is where we stood, It is a passage way leading
to the Orchestra seats + it costs $3.00 to stand there

My future father George, his brothers Jimmy and Peter. Three
ragged-arsed young immigrants, their futures yet unscored in an
America careering towards the Crash of '29, the great calamity
yawning just ahead like an apocalyptic Niagara, its coming
thunder still unheard above the roar of the Twenties. There they
stand, these brothers, under the boxes of the Vanderbilts, the
Astors, the Harrimans, the Julliards and J. P. Morgan, in a high

temple of art and wealth and privilege, in a frantic metropolis of B-movie speakeasies, in a country soon to be flayed by a blizzard of collapsing stocks and bonds. *Ladies will kindly remove their hats during the performance. Reserved Carriages may use the 39th Street, 40th Street and Broadway entrances on arrival. The Buffet is located on the Grand Tier Floor.*

In another part of the city on that November evening wasn't the young Duke Ellington raising a storm at The Cotton Club?

But those three young Irishmen know nothing yet of that nativity, that urgently American pulse and its mythologies. They're listening to Rosa Ponselle, to Ezio Pinza, to Giovanni Martinelli, to sounds they've never heard, words they don't need to understand. The plot is outlandish but the occasion magnificent. The music beats over them in passionate waves — as over me now — telling of relentless destiny, encounter, love and death, retribution and redemption. By day they casually work as house painters, signwriters, elevator operators. Sometimes on cold nights my father goes to the New York Public Library and transcribes poems of Yeats into a blank diary which, miraculously, will not be lost in time. Sometimes the three brothers skip work and spend a summer's day in Coney Island, touring the sideshows, gaping at the freaks, chasing the girls.

Jimmy, the eldest and the first to emigrate at the age of twenty in 1920, will never see Ireland again. He'll marry a girl named Leah Grimshaw in Long Island, of a family disapproving of Catholics and Irish Catholics particularly, though he will never again darken a church door once he's escaped the bitterly remembered clerics of his youth. He'll make his passion for grand opera his religion, scratching a living as a signwriter in Westhampton, accumulating a record collection of great voices, drinking most nights at The Patio. He will become outwardly assimilated but never content, watching as year by year the New York rich appropriate the foreshore, hardening into a bitter old age, in the end as unforgiving of his Long Island village as of the town he came from. Over the years letters from the homeland bring him word of clay on coffins: father and mother, sisters, a brother. Towards the end he'll write for photographs: The Old Bridge, Cook Lane, The Weir and Carrickbeg. Two years before he dies he'll almost make a visit back after fifty years. He'll get as far as JFK and then turn back, sending his American wife Leah instead.

By the time I get to Long Island he will be ten years dead. I'll stand with Leah over the parched grass under which his ashes lie. Later his daughter will come to Ireland, find the green river valley, the town, the house where her father's story began. She'll tell how he first brought her up to New York and the Met when she was eleven, how he could never fathom her love of jazz, how he never spoke of Ireland. Had he buried and sealed it in some dumb hole he'd dug inside himself?

All this waits to happen as the curtain rises at the Met in November 1927. Peter, beside him, will weather the Depression for a while, then come back to Ireland to marry Kathy Healy, his hometown sweetheart ('the best-looking girl in Carrick') before some rival snatches her and in spite of the unbending disapproval of his mother, a hard woman of the Victorian shopkeeper class who is also a secret drinker. He'll rejoin the town's brass band under his father's baton and play the trombone which later I will play myself. The one which now hangs on my wall and sympathetically vibrates to Verdi. Later Peter will switch to trumpet in dance bands, becoming a noted crooner in pub and ballroom. Old sidemen still remember the passion he put into his best song:

> Once I built a railroad, made it run,
> Made it race against time;
> Once I built a railroad, now it's done,
> Brother, can you spare a dime?

When his teeth start to go Peter will lay aside the trumpet and later take up alto sax, hitting the bottle hard until he dries out in his forties only to keel over on stage at fifty-three just as he counts the band (my mother on piano) into *La Cumparsita* in the Ormonde Hall on St Stephen's night in 1958. The dancers sent home in shock, their money handed back as they exit. Buried in his musician's dress suit: he couldn't stand brown burial habits, not to mention churches, hospitals or funerals. Kathy, who bore him nine children, will live to be a handsome eighty-seven, with stories of his binges, the trumpet or the dress suit in the pawnshop, the throwing of crockery. All told with laughter in the end.

The third brother standing there will be my father. He's twenty-one. After he returns to Ireland he'll always wear his hat like George Raft and in drink say things like 'No dice, brother!'

He stands utterly entranced by Rosa Ponselle. A year before he dies in 1973 he'll write to her through the American Embassy, reminding her of how she sang Leonora in *La Forza del Destino* at the Met in 1927, his first year in America. The daughter of an Italian immigrant and originally a child singer in vaudeville, she had made her spectacular Metropolitan début in 1918 as Caruso's choice in *La Forza del Destino*. Her 'handsome stage figure and golden voice' were a sensation, 'with a seamless sound from rich low contralto to an effortless top C and electrifying trills'. In 1937 the Met's in-house politics denied her a part she coveted. She had a nervous breakdown and packed it in for good. Her secretary will reply from Villa Pace in Baltimore in 1972, when she is seventy-five and a year before my father will come home from the pub one night to face his final coronary just after he'd sung *There's a long, long trail a-winding into the land of my dreams*:

My Dear Mr Coady,

Miss Ponselle is recovering from a severe illness and has asked me to thank you for your touching letter. Your devotion to opera struck a responsive chord — especially remembering those unpleasant times during the Depression. Miss Ponselle has asked me to send you her very best wishes and to file your letter with her 'very special' ones. She regrets that this letter will not carry her signature due to her illness.

But that's still far upstream on that November evening at the Met. When the Crash comes my future father will stand in breadlines until he finds a job assembling typewriters in the Underwood factory in Hartford. Dark mornings from a rooming house, long lines of bent heads through twelve-hour working days, the ceaseless prowl of elevated supervisors' cradles moving above the production line. Outside the gates, turned-up collars and beaten faces waiting for vacancies. One night he'll cough awake to blood on his pillow. That dark seed he had carried in his lungs from Ireland; that intimate acquaintance which will take his father and young sisters.

In the tangle of chance and choice every effect in turn becomes a cause. When I am a boy he will remember all this by the fireside, in his cups. The Hartford doctor's advice: *Get back to Ireland, young man.* The great storm on the passage home. His recovery under his mother's care. The dance he went to one night in the Foresters' Hall. The girl from Waterford playing the piano. Duke Ellington's 'Solitude' as they danced together. Their marriage and my own genesis, by circumstantial indirection out of blood on a pillow in Hartford, a place in which I'll find myself by chance in

1982, touring on an open Greyhound ticket when he's nine years dead. Remembering, I'll try to find the Underwood factory. Long gone, of course, with Highway 84 inexorably rolling through its vanished assembly lines, its distant tramp of factory hands, its muted tyranny of time and hooters and long dead overseers. I stand on the highway's margin, a tourist in sunshine pointing a camera at a factory which is no longer there.

A poem comes out of this: 'Assembling the Parts'. As the pen finds it on the page there is a jolt of recognition, the kind that's obvious once seen: within that mundane timetable word 'destination' the hooded arrest, the dark drum-roll of *destiny*.

In the long chain of consequence there are no absolute beginnings, no absolutely final endings. All things connect in time. Before she dies in 1994, an old nun in Carrick will invite me to the convent where she must vacate her music room and dispose of her treasures. She entered in 1926, the year my father went to America. Now, before she moves to a rest home after her stroke, she must offload her books, her sheet music, her bound Mozart sonatas, her old records. From the stack she hands me, all unknowing, an old 78: Rosa Ponselle and Ezio Pinza singing 'La Vergina degli Angeli' from *La Forza del Destino:*

> *May the Virgin of the Angels*
> *Within her mantle fold you,*
> *And all the holy angels*
> *In their keeping ever hold you.*

ALL SOULS

Somebody loves us all.
— Elizabeth Bishop

After dark bottles and hours of tracing
with two good friends in the month of all souls
at the crowded bar of the Carraig Hotel,
long ago known as the King's Head Inn
when cantered alarms of French invasion
had Carrick yeomen guarding the bridge;

    after the last of the rounds and yarning
    about the charms of the women of Cork
    about Plunger Maher and Sheet Metal's missus
    about Bugler Whalen and Butt o' Spuds
    about nights of promise in Ballylaneen
    about Lucius O'Neill who could converse in Latin,

        after wellworn jokes and our phallic favourite
        about the private N-Y tattoo of a patient
        that has the nurse guessing he's from the Big Apple
        until he invites her to stroke and see
        that he hails from Newtownmountkennedy —

yes, after helpless bouts of laughter
at the merest mention of Newtownmountkennedy,
proving the old ones are still the best ones
and truly there's no better gift in life
than laughter and none more profound in the end
except perhaps sleep, or music, or children
(which is what we've become in the course of our
    drinking)

after all this and more besides,
since time is up and we've homes to go to
in the heel of the hunt we're out in the fog
that mantles in mystery the cross above Bridge Street
where we part with safe home
                safe home
                    safe home.

Then I'm on my own and heading toward
the town clock salmon swimming above
the West Gate that's seen every soul who ever
set foot in this place for a thousand years

        including Cromwell and William of Orange
        Daniel O'Connell and Mary Spake Aisy
        Cough No More and Boil 'Em In Oil
        Féach Amach and *Pingin Fé Chloch*
        Peggy's Leg and Pull Through
        The Sleepy Tailor and All Is Well
        Red Spinner and Rattle the Latch
        Seán a Mham and *Fear Bocht*
        Blue Lookout and Hole in the Wall
        Hat o' Thrushes and Hot Fomentation
        Pigeon's Milk and Khyber Pass
        Laredo and Moscow and Oilcan and Oxo
        Bengal Lancer and Mary Game Ball —

on this grounded night I meet them all.

        There's old Dick Bromley drunk as a lord
        and fined in 1790 for leaving
        the whole town timeless for most of a month
        because he neglected to wind the clock,

and there's Mag Delaney at the West Gate
hearing her own last Act of Contrition
under the wheels of a Crossley Tender,

        and here's the Corpus Christi procession
        with incense and brass band and *Soul of My Saviour:*
            Which hymn would you like? asked Neddy Keevan.
            Him on the big drum, replied the young novice.

        There's my infant self in my mother's arms
        the night Guiry's garage became an inferno.

Then, as if led on by remembered heat,
I pick up the scent of deep fat frying,
and though it's hard to fathom north from south
my fogbound nose navigates my mouth
in to Ella's for black pudding and chips
    with yes to the salt, and yes to the vinegar
        before I reel out again in billows of steam

    just as the town clock looming above me
    out of the fog starts to strike out midnight
as it's done more or less for two hundred years.

        Is it a knell or a resurrection
    that stops me dead above Grey Stone Street
    on a night so blind I can't see my feet?

The clang overhead brings a host of phantoms
    out of the mist to drift by in the dark:
        the rogues and the desperate
        the ugly and beautiful
        the shawled and bareheaded
        the lost and the loving
        the drowned and the hungry
        the kind and the cunning
            the singers
            the suicides
            the blind
            and the lame

    with the sky on the ground
    and time's grammar astray
        real in their flesh
    under bell and salmon
        out of the dark
    they return in November
    to walk as they used to
    through the West Gate.

Orate Fratres
Pray brethern

for Edmund Kelly the fiddler
and Bartley Lenihan the cockle-carrier
for Mary Cody the baker of Castle Alley
and Sam Gray the pauper of Pyeman's Lane

for Pat Winton the breeches maker
          and Tim Byrne the weaver
for Ellen Lyons the cider woman
          and John Massey the brazier
for Kate Connors the washerwoman
          and John Brazel the hatter
for Ned Torpey the miller
          and Hannah Connell the huckster
for Brigid Kelly the blind piper
          and Rose Wade the servant
for Jim Haley the broguemaker
          and Liza Hickey the spinner
for Kate Hynes the mealwoman
          and Tom Campion the grocer
for Will Kennedy the innkeeper
          and Pat Buckley the ostler
for Andy Hennebry the blacksmith
          and Mag Ryan the breadwoman
for Con Ronayne the Newfoundlander
          and Grace Gaule the butcher
for Mary Thompson the cheesemonger
          and Isaac Toppin the nailer
for Patrick Lynch the schoolmaster
          and Jack Toomey the tailor.

A Thiarna an domhain maith dhóibh gach smál
O Lord of life forgive all faults
is réitigh leo go flaithiúil fial
and show your magnanimity

iad siúd a mhair faoi chlog 's bradán
to all who under bell and salmon
's a ghabh thar bráid an Gheata Thiar.
passed through the West Gate year by year.

For Bill Murphy the cooper
                    and Will Daniel the snuff grinder
for Kate Hunt the milkwoman
                    and Bob Kiely the joiner
for Nan Cooke the schoolmistress
                    and Will Crotty the craneman
for Jane Dwyer the ragwoman
                    and Tom Burke the distiller
for Charles Holliday the butter taster
                    and Tom Edmonds the tinker
for Will Connell the stay-maker
                    and James Wall the maltster
for Ellen Sheehan the shoemaker
                    and Jim Cronin the saddler
for John Hannon the chaise driver
                    and Garret Wall the skinner
for Maggie Rowe the haberdasher
                    and Tom Pike the sawyer
for John Stacy the printer
                    and Jack Sinnot the pavior
for Judy Stone the dressmaker
                    and Charles Byrne the waiter
for Jim Hayden the stonemason
                    and Will Kelly the glazier.

A Mháthair Dé coimeád cúntas réidh
O Mother of God keep ready account
ar an slua seo scáil ina n-aiséirí,
of this host of resurrected shades,
gach fear is bean a mhair cois abhann
all souls who saw the river flow

is a shiúil thar droichead le linn a saoil.
and crossed the old bridge in their day.

For Garret Russell the basket-maker
                and Jim Hayney the boatman
for Mary Sullivan the midwife
                and Thady Meehan the porter
for Harry Mathews the policeman
                and John Duggan the usher
for Ann Forrestal the gardener ·
                and Tom Flynn the drummer
for Tom McCarthy the dancing master
                and Bill Daniel the barber
for Kate Hogan the flax dresser
                and Francis Doyle the draper
for Tempest Knox the excise man
                and Peter Wells the tanner
for Mary Lamb the collar maker
                and James St John the turner
for Tom Stevenson the stocking weaver
                and James Ryan the scribe
for Ann Casey the woolwasher
                and Bill Magrath the size boiler
for Tom Shea the fisherman
                and Martin Fleming the friar
for Jill Minihan the button maker
                and Jack Johnson the dyer.

Bí linn, Naomh Cuan is Brógán,
Be with us, Cuan and Brógán,
ó thobar beannaithe Maothail thall;
from Mothel's blessèd well beyond;
beidh bláth ar gach aon chnoc is gleann
hill and glen will flourish while
an fhaid 's tá brúcht fíor uisce ann.
your wellspring gushes from deep down.

For John Shanahan the stone cutter
        and Ned Burke the slobber
for Nicholas Herbert the rector
        and Mat Finn the jobber
for John Dorney the horse breaker
        and Wat Aylward the carpenter
for Kate Butler the pedlar
        and Tom Fitman the thatcher
for Mickel Magrath the shovel maker
        and Mag Clancy the publican
for Ned Keeffe the limeburner
        and Tom Higgins the attorney
for Tadhg Driscoll the salt maker
        and Tim Damer the cowherd
for John Carshore the surgeon
        and Honor Phelan the cripple
for Ally Mahony the gingerbread woman
        and Mary Shea the seamstress
for Edmund Green the sieve maker
        and Nick Faoláin the priest
for Henry Hayden the watchmaker
        and John Power the proctor
for Mary Brennan the charwoman
        and Daniel Ryan the doctor.

Oremus
Let us pray

ar son gach n-aon,
for all of these,
Amen.

Garda na n-Aingeal ós ár gcionn,
Guard of Angels overhead,
stiúirigh gach sprid trí cheo na hoích',
steer all souls through fog of night,

treoraigh gach scáil trí gheata na ngrást
direct each shade through the gate of grace
ó chrosaire Shráid na Cloiche Liath.
beyond the cross of Grey Stone Street.

AS WE ARE NOW SO ONCE WERE THEY
WHO YET AWAIT THE JUDGEMENT DAY,
AS THEY ARE NOW SO WILL WE BE
UNTIL ALL MEET ETERNALLY.

With the bell's last overtone
the fog's maw swallows them

    as I muster my wits
    that are half astray

and through swirling vapours
start to feel my way

    listening for the Night Watch drum
    beating time in the Year of Blood

    reaching into the bag to eat
    as I guess my bearings and find my feet

    dodging the debris of the Temperance Club
    collapsing one morning just before dawn

past Thomas Cleary returned to sing
*Cathleen Mavourneen the grey dawn is breaking
the horn of the hunter is heard on the hill*

    breathing a prayer for the soul of the child
    lost in the fire at Peggy Brown's

past Bronco Ryan demonstrating the tango
at the Harriers' dance with a woman who's drowned

to the strains of the Ormonde Follies Orchestra
whose music sounds faintly away in the universe

>   past Annie Hayes pawning a pair
>   of cotton drawers for sevenpence-ha'penny
>   and Bid Healy redeeming a man's top coat
>   six years before the Titanic went down
> >   past the fifer's child sent to ask the pawnbroker
> >   *How much would you give on me father's flute?*

past Barrel Walsh years off from his cancer
with the Stardusters band as he bends to the mike
for a special request to sing *I'll be seeing
you in all the old familiar places*

>   and Harry Doherty soaring on clarinet
>   into the last chorus of Time After Time

past all souls plucking Michaelmas geese
with a snowfall of feathers about their knees
at the fowl-buyer's yard beside the Wide Lane

past Mother Baptist teaching me tables
and Prayers Before and After Communion
or me standing up in short pants on the desk
at the top of the class for command performance
after she calls for a song with the surety
the Coadys were always musical and I give
Down by the glenside I met an old woman
learned from my father before I was seven,
>   past Baptist recalling this when she's near ninety
>   and no two stones of the school still standing

past Tom the Bard in his bedroom hoping
for a night of ease from the cursèd leg
and Peggy on her knees presenting a list
as long as your arm to Our Lady and St Martin

asking blessings on all she can think of
and also on all of those she's forgotten

     past the young oak the Bard and I planted
     one day in the garden in '84
     past the boat grounded in cabbage and onions
     that he built himself to a passing chorus
     of God bless the work and When is the deluge?

       past Tony Curry giving as gospel
       the biggest flood ever in Carrick was the one
       that left the salmon on top of the town clock

     past summer days of Chuck Hackett stabbing
     eels in the stream behind Salt Yard Lane

past fog-lamped leviathans grinding down
at the blinded junction for Rosslare and Europe

     past Jody Carr and his four dogs listening
     to Gigli singing *Celeste Aida*
     in darkest midnight by Cider Lane

past Nanny Hogan in the aproned evening
washing the convent cows' bellies and udders
on Mill River steps at Thunderford Bridge

     past a meltdown of laneways and houses
     with their babies and corpses and asses and ferrets
     their pig's head and cabbage and bread and tea
     their shawls and sideboards and candlesticks
     their lovers and haters and hopeless cases
     their basins and kettles and Sacred Hearts
     their drunkards and saviours and daughters in trouble
     their pisspots and skillets and fishing nets
     their chancers and soldiers gone to the war
     their finches and dogs and darned long johns

past the depression worn in the limestone
lip of Clareen Well by immemorial
        knees of women bending with buckets

and the lost face and hands of the mason
who dressed the kerbstones in a perfect circle

        past backlit clusters of men and boys
        playing pitch and toss for head or harp
        around the door at Foley's forge

past the tide turning unseen in the river
and a pair of otters sliding over the weir

        past my grandfather leading the band
        from the opening day of Davin Park
        by houses whitewashed for the Eucharistic Congress
        and marching home to die in six months

past lifts of cheering on summer evenings
for young men leaping and clash of hurleys

        past the mad cock of Treacy Park
        who maintains it's morning just after midnight
        and rouses the dogs to argue the case

past Nellie Connors raising her glass with
Thanks be to God we're still above ground

        past Annie Roche rising her song
        about Napoleon overpowered
        at Moscow by the sleet and snow

past Maggie Grey in fur coat and headscarf
shuffling for bread and milk in the morning

past the last train down from Limerick Junction
announcing itself to the man at the gates

    past Johnny Cleary waking the dead
    with Oft in the Stilly Night and Bold Robert Emmet

        past the best hopes of the John Paul the Second
        Racing Pigeon Club snug on their perches

past Mikey Callaghan telling of tides
and boatmen and drownings before his aside
that he's a hardy eighty-five years strong
and riding a Raleigh that's seventy-one

    past Daisy Belle dressed on the day of her wedding
    and Bob Power hoisting a sack of spring salmon

        past Johnny Robinson back from the grave
        to re-spin a yarn about three tinkers frying
        sausages at a crossroads one Good Friday

past my great-grandmother's crucifixion
screaming the last of her four days' labour
at the birth of her death in the Workhouse ward

    then up the incline of the Poorhouse Field
    trying not to notice nameless clamour
    from the limbo of paupers locked in the dark

    averting my eyes from the blind girl standing
    with her two bastard children before the Guardians
    as they argue her pleas to be taken in

        and tasting the last
        of the salt and the vinegar
        on this eyeless night
        in the month of all souls

with a scatter of leaves
at my feet to remind me
I've hardly brushed more
than a branch or two
in the forested timescape
of all that was
or is now
or will be

here in a valley
of fathomless tidings
under the cairn
cresting Slievenamon.

Though I'm short of breath it's last lap now
past the silver birch we planted together
carrying every leaf of next summer
perfectly folded already in bud,

then in the front door and the hall with the Russian
icon of the Mother of God of Tenderness
and upstairs to check
on the innocent eyelids
of Niamh and Lucy and James
in their dreaming,

then in to the bedroom
to strip in the dark,

turn back warm coverlet
and slide in at last
to the drowsy embrace
and the whispered welcome

Were there many below in the town?

THINGS THEY SAY

(Besides Their Prayers)

The Longest Puck
Neddy Kelly lofted a ball
in the Davin Park
one evening.

The *sliotar* landed
in a passing train
and ended up in Limerick.

Meteor Shower
Wouldn't you think
they could have it
a bit earlier in the night?

Obituary
He never done nothin'
to no one.

Regatta Day
The band is out
and the tide is in.

Bad Backs
We're fed up of
festivals and funerals
and Munster Finals
with backs that were
cat melodeon.

Judgement
Shocking the way they broke into
the Court House
and shitted on
the judge's chair.

I wonder who had to clean it up
before the monthly sitting?

I didn't hear, but you may be sure
she wasn't a man with a wig.

Redundancy
The finest tool in town they say
but crippled with his back.

Uncoupling
He started up the chainsaw
in the middle of the night
and offered to make
two halves of the house.

The Big Picture
We look not merely forward
but outward
and beyond

the Chairman said in his speech
before the start of the bicycle race.

Rights
He's not supposed to be drinking,
he's not supposed to be smoking,
by rights he shouldn't be in it at all.

Marksman
How did such a harmless little man
make babies with a woman
the size of her?

Like shovin' a small sausage
up the Main Street
but with a deadly aim.

Pub Quiz
How many crows
can perch on the town clock?
How many stones in the weir?
How many salmon swam under the Old Bridge
in the last five hundred years?

Likewise
Some are wise
and more are otherwise.

Bottom Line
This is what life
is all about,
says Harry,
measuring the grave.

Last Word
What's the worst thing
a woman can say to a man
in three
two-letter
words?

Is
it
in?

FIVE AIRS
FROM AN OLDER MUSIC

At Dawson's Grave

after the Irish of Seán Clárach Mac Domhnaill 1691-1754

The original satire on Colonel James Dawson of Aherlow, Co Tipperary, is
one of the most savage pieces of invective extant in Irish literature. Following
its composition the poet was forced into hiding, reputedly in London.

Squeeze him, graveslab, and crush down into the clay
That bloated and blood-sucking bastard, Dawson the grey
Whose fame owed nothing to valour displayed on the field
Since hanging the poor was the height of his chivalry.

A byword his name, breathed far on the wind,
For the bolted door and the iron fist within,
In Aherlow glen in a gap below Galtee peaks
He harassed the people with hunger to bring them to heel.

This ground is the narrow plot now where Dawson is stretched
Who strode through the land and took pleasure in halters of
    hemp,
Widows and orphans he scattered in rags east and west —
May he dangle and dance over flames in a jig without end.

My prayer I send cantering after his coffined heels
Down to the hobstone of hell where he howls for relief.
May every ravenous mongrel from Cork to Bruree
Sniff a path to his grave and gnaw at his nose and his ears.

It's a pity the like of him did not choke on his shit
Along with John his son, that gormless git;
To atone for the dirt that he dealt when he had his way
May curs with the mange have his insides to taste and to tear.

Great was his gullet when he could gobble up fields
And heavy the heel he set on the necks of the weak;
Now he is spancelled forever and led to a feast
Of hunger and thirst with servings of fire for his meat.

He who was cocksure and swollen with gold in his day,
May his hoard be consumed in the gizzards of impotent heirs.
While maggots take a lease on his belly to settle and feed
May his spirit be scalded and seared beyond counting of years.

In his day he pissed on the laws of man and of God,
This jack-booted upstart with a pedigree less than his dog's.
Since he never tired of mocking the church and the saints
Why should he expect any entry at heaven's gates?

His gate never opened an inch before misery's plea,
He was deaf to all lamentation and blind to grief;
The poorest who foraged for firewood or berries to eat
Were flogged until blood ran in streams from shoulders to knees.

Press down, graveslab, on his gums and grimacing teeth,
On his eyes, his tongue, his pate, his prick and his feet,
On each limb and joint and slimy organ within,
To ensure that his like may never stand upright again.

Na Prátaí Dubha

From the traditional song/poem of the Great Famine still extant in Ring, Co Waterford and attributed to Máire Ní Dhroma of Baile na nGall, Ring, c. 1850. 'The mountain graveyard' is Reilig a' tSlé, west of Dungarvan on the road to Youghal.

The black potatoes scattered our neighbours,
Sent them to the poorhouse and across the sea;
They are stretched in hundreds in the mountain graveyard,
May the heavenly host take up their plea.

O God of Glory, save and answer us,
Loose our bonds and right our case,
Give us life from out your heart again
And level the poorhouse in every place.

If it was sin brought this penance down on us,
Open our hearts and banish gall,
Anoint our wounds with your spirit's healing
And heavenly host take up our cause.

Too little we hold you in our memory
With the dark of life and its *caoin* of woe,
Oh Jesus Christ, lift this cloud from us,
May we see your face as we come and go.

The poor of Ireland truck with misery
With the pain of death and the weight of grief,
Little children scream each morning
From hunger pains, with no bite to eat.

It can't be God that brought this down on us,
The starving scattered under freezing skies,
Or the poorhouse door bolted cold and dark on them
With wives and husbands set apart to die.

Snatched from them without compassion
Were the children raised by them in pride,
Famished waifs tasting soup of misery
And no mother there to ease their cries.

Alas, there are those endowed with wealth enough,
Who do not serve the King of Life,
They abuse the poor who never had anything
But constant labour for all their time.

From early morning they toil unceasingly
Each sweated day until dark comes on,
Little gain their best can earn for them
But cold dismissal and tumbled homes.

Oh King of Pity and blessèd Lamb of God,
Free us from this tormenting pall,
Don't let a single soul be lost to you,
You whose passion redeemed us all.

The King of Glory will surely answer them
And the Virgin Mary unbolt the door,
The twelve apostles will make good friends of them
To share in plenty for evermore.

That day will show the true heart of charity
With the King of Heaven handing out relief,
The light of lights and the sight of Paradise
Will repay the poor for this earthly grief.

Máirín de Barra

from the anonymous eighteenth-century Irish love song

O Máirín de Barra, all my senses you've taken
And left me a wraith among my own people.
When I lie down at night it is of you I'm thinking
And you are the hunger I rise with at morning.

I thought I could woo you with words and with kisses,
I thought books might win you, with vows pledged between us,
I hoped for your hand when the barley was springing
But I was alone when the new year was coming.

The ground where you move is blessed by your walking,
The air when you sing is sweeter than honey;
Warm is the coverlet over your sleeping
And lucky the man you will take to your pillow.

I'd walk any place just to be near you,
I'd cross any sea and not ask for one penny,
I'd leave all my people forever behind me;
You could raise me to life with one word of welcome.

All of my heart to you has been given
Since the feastday of Mary in the candlelit chapel,
More lustrous your eye than dew on young cornfields
And sweeter your voice than the note of the starling.

Peadar na Péice

after the Irish of Tadhg Gaelach Ó Súilleabháin 1715-1795

Tadhg Gaelach spent most of his life in the Waterford Déise. His wild youth included a spell in Cork Gaol for drinking the health of the Pretender. In later life he fervently repented of his former debauchery and was reborn as a composer of passionately religious Irish verse, published after his death (*Timothy O'Sullivan's Pious Miscellany*, Clonmel, 1810) and widely used and sung in Munster churches up to the Great Famine. Tradition has it that Tadhg died while at his prayers in *An Séipéal Mór* in Waterford. His fine Latin epitaph was a flourish of classical learning from his friend and fellow-poet Donncha Rua Mac Conmara (1715-1810). *Peadar na Péice* (Peter of the penis), from Tadhg's rakish period, has tended to be air-brushed from the official canon. Its joyously unbuttoned mode represents a mediaeval European genre.

Who hasn't heard of Peadar na Péice
Whose crozier caused such consternation?

Small wonder indeed that he'd be famous
With a staff so sound and strong and able,

Well designed with a roundy rim to it,
Silken smooth, and totally shameless;

Frolicsome too, and all set for raking,
Eagerly sniffing and desiring labour;

A firm upstanding flahoolock wattle
To drive out all lovelorn frustration,

Spirited, sporting, vigorous, hairy —
A stayer of proven reputation.

Better to root than a snouting sow is
And able for any excavation,

A vigorous bough with well-hung apples,
Honey-filled and ripe for raiding,

With a tender well of juices dripping
And every drop on tap for draining.

None better to solve any lovesick crisis
Than such a practised mediator,

Like well-tuned pipes with a chanter able
To seduce and soothe the whole female nation.

What magic spear of Fianna Éireann
Could open doors like this persuader?

For nowhere under the sun was found
Such a skilled and subtle negotiator.

No sultry matron or flighty filly
Would turn down such an invitation

And poor oul' wans were worn out praying
For news of this lusty lad's location,

So when 'twas rumoured to be in Dingle
A pilgrimage was in the making

And though the way was rough and the going hard
Away from home they soon were faring

Thinking to get there in time to spare it
From burn-out or hyper-ventilation,

Hoping to outflank young wantons
Until they reached the edge of Béara

Where they found the crack was up to ninety
With brandy and punch and wild gyration

And brazen straps taunting withered crones
With dudeens their only consolation.

In the end the women took to fighting
Bar one who sized up the situation,

Slipped aside and seized her chance
For a red-hot ride till dawn was breaking —

A woman of sense, knowing love, not war,
Was the whole point of Peadar na Péice.

Tadhg's Epitaph

by Donncha Rua Mac Conmara 1715-1810

After the Latin inscription over the grave of Tadhg Gaelach Ó Súilleabháin at Ballylaneen, Co Waterford.

THADDEUS HIC SITUS EST, OCULOS HUC FLECTE VIATOR,
ILLUSTREM VATEM PARVULA TERRA TEGIT.
HEU! JACET EXAMINIS, FATEM IRREVOCABILE VICIT
SPIRITUS E TERRA SIDERA SUMMA PETIT . . .

Tadhg lies here, shed tears for him oh traveller:
Here is a poet and seer in mere earth clothed.
Alas for one brought low by time's sure arrow
Though up among the stars his spirit's risen.
Who now will sing the deeds and men of Erin?
Our muse is dumb, its ancient voice extinguished.
He left us with his poems to mourn his going,
A victor bearing gifts of his own making.
The Lord of all was subject of his praising
Who now is choiring high among the angels.
Let the muses weep, whose favourite has ascended,
A hero taken, leaving all the land in silence.
The peace he sought, may he in heaven share it
And find his place within the Father's kingdom.

THE USE OF MEMORY

James Coady c. 1815-1895
the old boatman of the Suir;
grandfather and guardian of the abandoned child.

|

James Coady 1848-1915
boatman of the Suir and the Delaware;
who left his son abandoned
and wrote the Philadelphia letter.

|

Michael Coady 1876-1932
the abandoned child.

|

George Coady 1906-1973
his son;
who witnessed the letter's arrival and rejection.

|

Michael Coady 1939-
grandson of the abandoned child.

The Letter

for James Coady, lost father of my grandfather

1

If there can be some
redemption in the word
then let this telling reach
across the silence
of a hundred years
in Oven Lane.

About your feet upon the earthen floor
let me find the child who will
out of the slow unravelling
become my grandfather
and in the curtained room
your young wife Mary Ager
still beside an infant
bound with her in rituals
of laying-out and prayer.

This dark hour's nativity
will shape and scar your destiny
and in the unformed future
cast its shadow over hearts
that will engender me;
in time it will call up
this impulse
and these words.

Let me try to know you
in the anguish of that hour

a man of no importance
trapped in a narrow place,
enmeshed in desperate circumstance
as at the whim of some
malignant puppeteer.

The image holds the lane,
its stench, the fetid hovels
crowding down toward
the quayside of the Suir
where kinship and compassion
resurrect in time upon the page
the murmured solidarity
and flickering of candles
about the human face
of piteous travail.

2

A hundred years and I will come
to try the lane for echoes

the coughing and the crying
of children in the dark,
the nameless incarnations
of love and grief and hunger
where the river flows
coldly past.

These broken walls were witness
to your leaving, whether
in morning sun or rain,
your firstborn child still sleeping
when you left him,
the dark-shawled blessings
from the doorways of a lane
you'd never see again.

3

What I know has come to me
out of dead mouths:
through the barefoot child
left with your father,
the old boatman, and from
the mouth of my own father,
that child's son.

A life I'll never know
is buried with you
in a place I'll never find:

a generation turned before
the morning of the letter
sent to find your son
become a man
with children of his own.

Out of the maze of circumstance,
the ravelled tangle of effect and cause,
something impelled you,
brought you finally
to bend above
the unmarked page —

an old man
in some room in Philadelphia
reaching for words to bridge
the ocean of his silence,
pleading forgiveness of the child
of Oven Lane.

4

Silence was the bitter
answer you were given
every empty day
until you died:

by a breakfast table
my child father
watched your son unseal
his darkest pain,

saw the pages torn and cast
in mortal grief and anger
out of an abandoned child's
unspeakable heart-hunger
into the brute finality
of flame.

5

Now all of these
have gone into the dark
and I would try again
to reconcile the hearts
of which my heart's compounded
with words upon a page.

I send this telling out
to meet the ghosts
of its begetting,
to release it from stone mouths
of Oven Lane.

from Oven Lane, 1987

This is the use of memory:
For liberation — not less of love but expanding
Of love beyond desire, and so liberation
From the future as well as the past.

— T. S. Eliot

I

The basket weaver is the man who holds the key. On one day, of many such days, I call to his workshop in New Lane. Joe Shanahan is also the sacristan of my parish church of St Nicholas, only yards from his workshop. On such days we chat a while as he sits at his craft, bending and weaving willow rods into a basket which he rounds and shapes upon his lap. His apprentice Barry Torpey is repairing a willow chair. I have stepped into a tableau that could be from any century, any culture. Joe's hands are strong and deft; in a lifetime of shaping, the hands that weave have in turn been moulded by the baskets they have woven. These are also the hands of the man who for a generation has tolled the parish bell for Mass, Angelus, funeral; the hands which have prepared chalice and water, communion bread and wine, incense and book. Ninety feet above our heads is the church bell in its granite belfry tower. For all of his adult life Joe has been linked to the gravity of its rope, as generations have been attuned to its reverberation.

We chat a while in the workshop in New Lane, among sheaves of sally rods, finished laundry baskets or herring crans, a half-made crib for some child on the way, a picnic hamper ordered from America. Then, the nuanced protocol of smalltown courtesy observed, Joe leaves his work aside and crosses the street with me to unlock the church sacristy, a high and spacious room of dim light and sacral silence. There is an elaborate ritual of keys allowing access in turn to other locks and keys until, finally, a safe door swings open on the shelves which hold the parish registers that survive since 1784. Joe leaves me and returns to his basket weaving, and I am alone in a hush of place and testament and time, the silence underscored by the slow beat of the pendulum clock in the corner. A heavy door stands between me and the body of the parish church in which I was baptised, as were family generations before me in this and previous churches on the site for two hundred years. Here, at my imagination's elbow, is the penned sacramental chronology of a whole community, the books more enduring than the buildings they outlasted, their Latin entries the only surviving testament to a vanished host of lives.

Some things must be tasted slowly, reflectively. Their potency is cumulative. Over hours, days, weeks, I learn the profound *gravitas* of this intimate communal lexicon. There are no indexes to the volumes: the Latin formulae recording details of baptisms and marriages are stratified here in the order of their happening from day to day, month to month, generation to generation. How many destinies are cryptically coded here? Perhaps two hundred thousand of the dead? Sometimes the entries include revealing glosses: a now vanished local placename, a tinker marriage identified in Latin (*vagrantes*), an illegitimate birth, a foundling, a nuptial dispensation between cousins. For most of the nineteenth century the parish priest rather than one of the curates invariably officiates at a Main Street baptism or marriage, and the offering often noted under the entry is likely to be in pounds rather than shillings and pence. Otherwise the poor give what they can. What became of the infant of Salt Yard Lane whose baptism in 1859 prompted the marginal comment *Promises to pay one shilling*?

The individual human transience of two centuries of lives densely manuscripted here dismays the heart, yet each entry also embodies a quality of its own immediacy still fluid on the page. There, in the hurried Latin flourish of a dead priest's living hand, I can almost touch the particularity of a February day in 1876 when an infant, one day old, was brought here and christened Michael.

More than a century later I stand here above the page, my own presence mysteriously enabled within the sacramental moment of this child's initiation, the moment of naming, of water and candles and chrism, of pen and ink and page. My imagination enters a mode for which I coin the word *presequence* — a knowing return to a seminal moment in the past from its own future. Here I discover myself already nested in the possible. In the converging future of this baptismal moment, out of the mysterious interweave of human choice and chance, I will become a grandson of that infant of Oven Lane who is cradled here under the sponsor's shawl. The priest who has baptised the child dips pen in ink and writes in the book. The ink begins to dry.

This child's birth foreshadows a family story out of which, over a century later, I fashion a poem. The process of the poem's making has brought me here to the silence of the sacristy. But that poem, when I have completed and published it, will not rest easy. In a wholly unforeseen interaction of art and life it will cause a lost part of its own story to be uncovered in America. 'Poetry,' wrote

Auden, 'makes nothing happen.' Not true for me, in this case. All of this has to do with the process of memory and the flux of time, with human destinies and the written word, with what is hidden, and what is revealed. The purpose of genealogy should not be the neat assembly of pedigree culminating smugly in self, but its exact opposite: the extension of the personal beyond the self to encounter the intimate unknown of others in our blood.

◄⧕ ⧔►

Carrick-on-Suir lies in a rich pastoral setting at the tide-head of the Suir, one of the 'Three Sisters' river system of southeast Ireland, in a landscape whose character has evoked comparison with that of the Loire. The town's south Tipperary borderline location ensured a diverse context of historical contact and interaction with the adjacent counties of Waterford and Kilkenny. I have lived here all my life. The landscape and human timescape of valley, river and town constitute my personal cosmos, my given commonwealth of imagination. Five miles to the north-west the fabled Slievenamon (*Sliabh na mBan*, 'mountain of the women') benignly overviews the valley. At the mountain's foot is the ruined castle of Kilcash, whose vanished glory was the subject of the classic eighteenth-century Gaelic lament of that name translated by Frank O'Connor in *Kings, Lords and Commons*. O'Connor claimed that the poem was a favourite of Yeats, who had Butler of Ormonde blood in him, and that the poet had a hand in its translation.

Across the river Suir and seven miles to the south in County Waterford are the dark glacial lakes of the Comeragh mountains, rich in Gaelic tradition. The lush river valley between Slieve-namon and the Comeragh foothills holds some of the most fertile land in all Ireland, but my story is not of land, since my people never owned any. The town (*Carraig na Siúire*, 'rock of the Suir') was a Norman creation, dominated, like the whole region, by the Butlers of Ormonde. The Butler castle still commands the river whose historical centrality as the highway to and from the wider world remained valid until the nineteenth century. The town's still surviving fifteenth-century bridge — for centuries the first bridge upstream of the estuary — made it strategically important, and its pivotal location at the tide-head of the river made it the historical nexus of trade and navigation between the larger upriver town of Clonmel and the city of Waterford some twenty miles downstream.

Carrick reached a peak of prosperity in the eighteenth century through the specialised weaving and dyeing of woollen cloth, with the town then holding twice its modern population of some five thousand souls. The common vernacular was Irish and the eighteenth-century community hosted some Gaelic scholarship and scribes as well as boasting a theatre, a military band, six pipers (one a blind girl) and a dancing master, a printing press and the publication of books in Irish and English. Hundreds of young men from the town migrated annually from the port of Waterford to the great cod-fishery of Newfoundland, called in the vernacular *Talamh an Éisc*, 'the fishing ground'.

Carrick's primary identity as a river town is still asserted in the weather-vane salmon surmounting its eighteenth-century town clock, but the mature river, once central to the community's life and economy, is now its dreaming soul, winding dimly through the communal unconscious as it slips under the bridges and past the quays. Now the only time the river asserts authority and power is when it overfloods its banks or when it suddenly drowns a man or child or woman, and the few remaining cotsmen who bear the knowledge of its floods and tidal currents, its backwaters and islands, put out their salmon nets to fish for a corpse.

Decline and endemic emigration set in with the the Act of Union in 1800 but, based upon the rich agricultural hinterland, a strong and stable class of mainly Roman Catholic merchants and shopkeepers consolidated their marketing and distributive position through the nineteenth century. The richest tracts of outlying countryside had historically been the power-base and domain of Protestant ascendancy and Big House. The rising Catholic mercantile class of the town led and oversaw the language shift, with the co-operation of their church. It is recorded that an itinerant Methodist preacher gave a 'tolerable' sermon in the Irish language on the Main Street in 1801, and the town and hinterland were bilingual until the Great Famine, but the utilitarian agenda of the emerging Catholic middle class required the abandonment of the native language and its immemorial cultural traditions, the dispossessed Gaelic world by then associated with poverty, oppression and backwardness. The grey orthodoxies of Victorianism penetrated deeply, persisting well into this century and eroding only gradually even after the achievement of political independence. In my own youth in the 1950s that telling Victorian label 'respectable' was still a common part of the town's colloquial code of class distinction.

My people are in there somewhere in the streets and laneways of this small Irish town clustered on both sides of a river. Men of no property, no Last Wills and Testaments: weavers, boatmen, artisans — townsmen all. They leave no record other than memory and oral tradition, and the women who bore their children are little more than names. All are briefly noted in the parish registers, and in the state record of births, marriages and deaths which began in 1864. Their graves are for the most part unmarked. But there is the rich and fascinating process of human memory and transmission; what it reveals, what it suppresses, what it reshapes. We are each given a darkly woven basket of inheritance, but it comes open-ended into our hands.

My father was a compulsive raconteur of family history and anecdote; it is only in retrospect that I have come fully to recognise the richness of his narrative gift and wish that I had listened more carefully, before his stories ended in the silence of the grave. During my childhood he often recalled a dramatic scene out of his own early experience. He remembered from his boyhood the arrival during breakfast one morning of a mysterious and wholly unexpected letter. It came to his father from a man who had left Ireland for America thirty or so years before and who had not been heard from in all the years since his departure.

This letter had come to my grandfather Michael from his long lost father, and it was some kind of plea for forgiveness. Although he was only a young child when he witnessed it, my father never forgot the drama of the letter's arrival and the response of my grandfather who read the pages, tore them into pieces and flung them with bitter finality into the fire. All his life Michael Coady believed that his father had abandoned him, and he never forgave the man. So painful was the memory of having been a deserted child that he never spoke of it, and the lost father in America who had reached out after all the years in an attempt to be reconciled with his son never received a reply. The book, it seemed, was closed.

Why then, should that dimly remembered story of the letter return to trouble my imagination a full century after the story began and years after my own father was dead? Why did it obsess me into making a poem which attempted to reconcile the dead in kinship and compassion?

There was an inheritance here which had returned to waylay my imagination, now that I had children of my own. A deeply personal story, but also one of fathers and sons, with archetypal resonances bearing upon moral obligation and the imperatives of kinship within my culture. The story's tangle of individual human destinies was also a tiny fragment of the great epic drama of migration from Ireland to America — that vast human enterprise of millions which, remarkably, has been so little articulated in a literature on either side of the ocean.

But above all the story's compelling potency lay in the very fact that it held so many questions. My grandfather had been deeply wounded and embittered by this unspoken — because unspeakable — childhood trauma of abandonment by his father following upon his mother's death. What had happened to my great-grandfather in America? What circumstances there brought him finally to write the letter? How long thereafter did this shadowy figure in America cling to the faint hope of some reply from the son whose forgiveness he had sought from an ocean away? If there was moral blame to apportion, then whose was the deeper guilt — the man who abandoned his child, or the child, grown a man, who could not forgive his father but left him to die with silence as his only response? We shape our children, for good and ill, out of our own dark shaping. Could this bitter inheritance have indirectly marked my own father, child of the abandoned child, and in its generational turn could it have even marked myself in ways of which I was scarcely aware?

There is something persistently enduring and unquiet about an unforgiven wound within the imperative context of kinship and its blood bonds. In the emotional archaeology of family the psychic scar of such a wound can be passed on beyond its own time to fester darkly within the sensibilities of its inheritors. I cannot remember exactly when or how the compulsion began to probe, explore, explain. Where lies the absolute genesis of anything? I could say my poem began writing itself in Oven Lane with a woman's death more than a hundred years ago. Nested within every beginning lie earlier beginnings and endings. Every past has seeded its own future. Every future will become a past for other futures.

Though I began by resisting such a fanciful notion, in the writing of the poem and in what followed from it the feeling grew that others were shadowing my shoulder, that I was in some way a medium through whom the unresolved pain of the past strained to be redeemed through the mystery of the word and its utterance. That fabled potency of the word would finally lead me to repossess the lost American part of the story.

❧ ❧

My great-grandfather, so my father thought, had left Ireland after his wife had died in childbirth. He had left his only son Michael in the care of his own father, the child's grandfather, an old boatman on the river. The boy was never to see his father again. The single fateful letter which arrived some thirty years later may have come from Philadelphia, and it told of remarriage there and of a second family.

In the poem I fixed upon moments of crisis and tried to reconstruct, understand, reconcile. The scenario could have come from Dickens: the woman dying in childbirth; the man leaving for America; the child left behind. Years on, the old man in Philadelphia writing a letter; the drama of its arrival, bitter rejection and destruction over a breakfast table in Ireland; the sender waiting in Philadelphia for a reply which never came, and dying there, unforgiven. Every writer knows the mysterious addition of unexpected things emerging on the page. As I wrote my way through its drafts, the poem became more than the exploratory articulation of the family narrative, with its mystery and pain. Its writing discovered something else in process: some paradigm for the mystery of the written word itself. I was invoking a poem of reconciliation within which I was also explicitly present as a writer, scripting the poem I invoked. As my great-grandfather in America had once bent over the blank page, so I found myself struggling to reply with words upon a page, three generations on.

Even as I wrote intuitively I also searched for recorded facts. It was only when I began my exploration of the parish registers unlocked for me by Joe Shanahan the basket weaver that I discovered that my great-grandfather had lived in Oven Lane — one of a network of alleyways that represent historical rights of way leading from Main Street down to the quayside of the Suir. Oven Lane is believed to have been named from the existence there of a public oven and kiln for drying corn in former centuries. I remember the frisson of discovery on finding the location noted under the entry recording my grandfather's baptism. My father had not told me this. Had he known and deliberately suppressed the fact, or could it have been withheld from him by his own father?

For my grandfather Michael in his adult years to have acknowledged Oven Lane as his birthplace would within his time have carried a stigma of shame. The word 'lane' evokes connotations of green rusticity in England. In Victorian Ireland a lane meant a fetid alleyway of slum dwellings and the word is invariably and painfully associated with the squalor and misery of the past. Victorian orthodoxy viewed poverty as moral malfunction: the poor were so not because they had no money or no work but because of their fecklessness, their laziness, their innate inferiority. The poor were to blame for their own poverty; to suffer it was also to be deeply branded with its shame.

Although the slums have vanished people in my town still recoil from using the word 'lane' as an element in naming a personal place of residence. The very word is erased and substituted for in a tacit social consensus to lay its ghosts; an Oven Lane address may even still choose to redefine itself semantically and socially as South Main Street.

For me the specific identification of Oven Lane with the family story gave my imagination focus and sustenance. An archaeology lay hidden in the name and in the site, waiting to be read or felt. The slum houses were gone but outlines remained: a bricked-in window in a wall, a faintly discernible lintel where once had been a doorway through which lives had come and gone. Below the lane the tiding river and the ancient bridge were unchanged. I walked lane and quayside in daylight and in darkness while I searched out whatever facts the records held.

I found that my great-grandfather James was born in 1848 — a Famine child — and married Mary Ager, a servant and the daughter of a shoemaker, in 1874. They both marked the register as illiterates. James Coady was a boatman on the river, probably working with his father in ferrying goods as part of the tidal trading to and from Waterford and the horse-drawn barge traffic to Clonmel. It was in Oven Lane that the couple's first child, Michael, was born in 1876. He was soon followed by Patrick, who died in infancy. In late 1879 a third child, Thomas, was born.

Then, in February 1881, Mary Coady, again pregnant, contracted anthrax, a serious bacterial infection of livestock that can occasionally spread to humans and prove fatal. After fourteen days in the grim public ward of the Workhouse hospital, four of them in labour, she died on an aborted birth. She was thirty-five. Dr James R Murphy of the town had made a formal complaint in 1873 regarding the treatment of some pregnant women by the resident Workhouse physician. His letter to the Board of Guardians specified abuses and gross neglect and concluded with a passionate 'God save the poor!' The only result of Dr Murphy's formal protest had been the loss of his post as apothecary to the Poor Law Guardians. The Workhouse stood until the 1920s, was partly burned during the Civil War and subsequently looted by the townspeople for its stone, its slates, its timber. A virile local authority housing estate now stands on the site. I live beside it in what was colloquially called the Poorhouse Field.

I don't know where James Coady's wife, my great-grandmother Mary, was buried: she may lie in a nearby field of anonymous humps and hollows which was the Workhouse graveyard. In autumn I walk there with my wife and children to gather blackberries and sloes for jam making.

Mary Coady had died in excruciating suffering less than seven years after her marriage. The youngest child, Thomas, aged two, died of fever ten months later. Only the first born, five-year-old Michael, who would become my grandfather, remained in Oven Lane with his father. The 1880s was a time of agricultural depression and consequent distress in town and countryside, with the bitter struggle of the Land War accelerating. The winter of 1881 had been harder than any in living memory; in January of that year the river froze. Joseph Ernest Grubb, a public-spirited

Quaker merchant in the town who controlled much of the river trade from Waterford, got up a subscription to aid the poor, some of them, he wrote, 'subsisting on field turnips boiled in water . . . with even tradesmen begging for employment as stonebreakers.' With the aid of his sisters in Birmingham he collected £200 in England in addition to £100 subscribed locally. The local chapter of the Society of St Vincent de Paul constantly issued appeals on behalf of those from among the destitute whom it categorised as 'the respectable poor'. For those in dire need there was the cold comfort of whatever Victorian charity might offer and beyond that the ultimate spectre of the Workhouse.

My grandfather Michael was about eight years old when his widowed father turned his back on Oven Lane and left for America. Family tradition is silent on how James Coady mustered his passage-money, whether he set out alone or with others, whether he ventured first downriver to Waterford or by train to Queenstown in Cork before he faced the voyage to the New World. The boy in Oven Lane was left in the care of his grandfather until his father might send for him from America. James Coady's father, the old boatman who was to be the boy's only guardian, was also named James and lived in Hayes's Lane, now closed and part of the rere of Bourke's Drapery, Main Street. I surmise that this old man, born around 1815, was probably the last native speaker of Irish in my direct paternal line. There is a whisper that he took some part in the abortive Young Ireland Rising of 1848.

The weeks, months, years that followed the emigrant's departure brought only a bewildering silence from America, with the boy growing up in Carrick as a virtual orphan of the lanes. The material and emotional deprivations of that childhood abandonment left deep and unforgiving scars.

In 1887 Michael's grandfather was taken into the Wadding Charity, Castle Street, a home for 'poor Roman Catholic persons of either sex born in the parish'. The arrangement was part of a deal whereby the Main Street drapery merchant Patrick Bourke (a trustee of the Wadding house and a town commissioner) closed Hayes's Lane to public access and acquired it as part of his property. The Wadding charitable institution had been set up in 1756 under a trust established by a Catholic of the town named Thomas Wadding after he emigrated to Spain. The bristling code of rules included one which obliged the inmates to gather nightly at seven o'clock in winter and nine in summer to offer prayers for the soul of the founder.

The institution's surviving Minute Books show that in 1888 the Trustees, who included the local parish priest, held a special meeting at which they agreed to allow the boy Michael Coady into the house nightly to sleep with his grandfather there — a highly irregular arrangement for such a rule-bound institution and one that starkly reveals the child's isolation and homelessness. Whenever I pass that ruined building now I am haunted by the dark nights the boy must have spent there, sharing a bed with his grandfather, surrounded by the night smells and groans of the overcrowded institution; an orphaned child confined amongst the debility and dementia of the aged and destitute.

Yet somehow Michael Coady managed to attend the Christian Brothers' school, where he continued until he was taken in as a thirteen-year-old apprentice shop boy in Bourke's Drapery, one of the most prominent establishments in the town. However Dickensian and regimented such a live-in apprenticeship was, it nevertheless signified the basic material security of assured food and shelter. Most live-in apprentices were not only unpaid for their first five years but were required to pay fees for the privilege and to live semi-monastic lives.

Family tradition remembers that the Christian Brothers had intervened on Michael Coady's behalf, appealing to Patrick Bourke to grant the boy the apprenticeship without requiring fees and to allow their bright pupil to continue his schooling through part of it. The merchant may have felt some particular responsibility for the orphan, having contrived to close and acquire Hayes's Lane in the deal which transferred young Michael's grandfather and only guardian to the Wadding house. Yet within its time the boy's induction as an apprentice at the prestigious Main Street emporium was an unusually liberal arrangement. Compared to the common lot of children of the lanes, and especially of orphaned ones, Michael Coady might consider himself fortunate. Bourke's Drapery probably saved him from the Workhouse and gave him a tentative but subsequently significant foothold on the threshold of middle-class opportunity.

What this Main Street matrix of Victorian security lacked utterly for the boy was any emotional sustenance in his growing years. From the early death of his mother and younger brothers and the bewildering disappearance of his father, Michael's primary experience of life from the age of five had been of traumatic loss, abandonment and loneliness. Bourke's Main Street drapery meant food and shelter and a ladder to 'respectability', but it also meant an unremitting regime of cold rules and conformity. The utter lovelessness of the boy's growing up was relieved only by the bond with his institutionalised grandfather, up to the old man's death at the Wadding Charity. Michael, then aged nineteen, was present at that death in 1895. He had come to love the old boatman in place of the father who had abandoned him and he would, in time, name his own first-born son in the old man's memory. In my time old rivermen could still point to the location of Coady's Slip, the mooring place, now marked by stone boatsteps from the quayside, from which old James Coady plied the river trade before and after the Great Famine.

⌇⌇

Bourke's records show that Michael completed his apprenticeship in the year of his grandfather's death in 1895 and was allowed a salary of £10 per annum. However, he left suddenly in the following year: family tradition maintains that he was dismissed because he had slipped out one night to play the fiddle at a rural house dance at Crehana, in the town's County Waterford hinterland, and found his employer waiting for him in his room when he climbed back in through the window in the small hours of the morning.

Yet this orphan child of Oven Lane who became my grandfather had somehow managed to acquire an education and some musical accomplishment. He eventually became a skilled law clerk and a prominent figure in Carrick life, led orchestras, and conducted the town's brass band, even as I do now myself. Following the introduction of proportional representation he would become widely noted in the wider region as a skilled supervisor at election counts. In 1899 he had made a significant socio-economic leap from his origins by marrying a daughter of the relatively prosperous boot making and shopkeeping Conway family of Main Street. Oven Lane festered only yards from the gaslit town centre with its strong Catholic merchants and small shopkeepers, but between the Main Street and the lane lay an almost unbridgeable gulf of class.

The marriage, however, was not to be a happy one. My grandmother Minnie Conway was a stern, pious and practical woman, copperfastened in Victorian shopkeeper certainties of thrift, sobriety and purgatives as the essential keys to material and moral salvation. Though he remained a public conformist in the matter of religious observance, my grandfather was deeply anti-clerical (as I know from an unguarded letter to one of his sons which survives) and became a heavy drinker with a disposition towards melancholia, a passion for music and books, and an inability to make money. His wife once took a hatchet and smashed his fiddle — perceived symbol for her of all his domestic irresponsibility — when he returned from a friend's house, late for dinner, one Christmas. He reacted by flinging the family's festive pudding across the room. So my father vividly remembered from his childhood, recalling a Christmas Day of tears.

My grandfather Michael was to die of tuberculosis at the age of fifty-six in the same upper bedroom of his wife's house in Main Street in which I was later to be born. In her old age his daughter-in-law Kathy Coady recalled for me how, as a young woman, she visited and spoke to him only hours before he died in that room on All Souls Night in 1932. He had dreamed, he told her, that he could hear the brass band playing the Dead March from *Saul*. Across the grey rooftops, in their band room, the men he had conducted for years and brought to national competitions were in fact rehearsing the sombre cadences of *Saul* in anticipation of his funeral — struggling to get it right, as an old brassman told me, without his direction.

The funeral of the late Mr Michael Coady, law clerk, Carrick-on-Suir, on Thursday evening was the largest and most impressive seen in Carrick for some years. About 2,000 people walked in the cortège from St Nicholas Church to Carrickbeg Friary, where the interment took place. The members of the Carrick-on-Suir Brass and Reed Band carried the coffin to and from the hearse. The band played the Dead March from St Nicholas Church to Carrickbeg. Deceased had been prominently identified with the band for the past thirty-five years. The members of the Carrick Social and Literary Club, of which deceased was Secretary, walked four deep behind the hearse. The legal profession in Carrick was represented by Messrs M. J. Quirk, P. Davin, P. Verrington, and James Power, solicitors.

The orphan of the lanes had earned himself a big send-off from the town. Buried with him was the trauma of his Oven Lane childhood, the suppressed memory of the lost father in America and the years of silence until the arrival of the letter which he had bitterly rejected. The writer of that letter was for me the one in deepest shadow. Even as I worked on, completed and published my poem I knew nothing of his life in America. His very christian name had not been known to my father, who was his grandson — a fact that tellingly indicates the hurt silence surrounding the story.

How might I uncover the lost life of James Coady in America

and try to unravel the mystery of his abandonment of the child who became my grandfather? Somewhere an ocean away, a century away, there must be some public record of the man. Could it be found? He was one utterly insignificant figure among millions, his story only one of countless others. I did not yet know exactly when he had left Ireland, or to which part of America he had gone. The only lead I had was my father's recollection that the letter, which arrived when he was a boy in the early years of the century, may have come from Philadelphia. All hung upon the fragile thread of my dead father's childhood memory. If Philadelphia was a misdirection then my quest amounted to a hopeless floundering in the vast human and spatial landscape of the Irish diaspora.

The poem was first published by David Marcus in his renowned New Irish Writing page of *The Irish Press* and later revised and reprinted in 1987 under the title 'The Letter' in the collection from The Gallery Press which I named *Oven Lane*. Still the matter would not rest easy, as if in some mysterious way the poem had already activated its own search and field of force. Through Hugh Ryan, an old Carrick bookman and friend, I learned of an expert Irish-American genealogist named Eileen McConnell who lives in Maryland. The element of serendipity enters: a few years before this Eileen and her husband Ken had been on a touring holiday in Ireland and happened upon the Carrick-on-Suir area through a misdirection. When they arrived in the town Hugh Ryan the bookman and assistant at Bourke's Drapery was the first man they chanced to meet and speak with.

I sent Eileen McConnell a copy of my poem, with whatever context of recorded fact I knew, and she too was quickly drawn into this tale of bitter disconnection between Ireland and America, this legacy of pain between a father and a son. I was asking her to attempt the near impossible in trying to uncover the lost life from the slimmest of leads, but we could only set out in hope, fixing our initial sights on Philadelphia in the 1880s, in search of a man named James Coady.

So began, over the course of two years, a long and often baffling and frustrating quest, and a voluminous transatlantic correspondence. Eileen McConnell lives quite close to the National Archives in Washington, but never met a more frustrating search, with numerous obstacles, false leads and blanks. It was a search in which creative hypothesis was necessarily often invoked along with the systematic combing of street directories, census records, newspapers, indexes of births, marriages, deaths . . .

Employing a professional researcher in America would in the normal course have been beyond my means even if I could have found the right person to commission. The induction of Eileen McConnell as an enthusiastic ally in my quest was a pivotal piece of good fortune for me and part of the continuing pattern of seren-dipity. To her invaluable experience and expertise Eileen added a personal interest in the story I asked her to pursue, and she under-took the work voluntarily. Miraculously, and piece by piece, the outlines of the American story began to emerge, coming to me fragmentarily and out of sequence, as she tracked down clues and investigated possibilities with a dogged persistence, devotion and skill which complemented what had by now become my own obsession. Every letter from her which landed in my porch held the exciting prospect of revelation; a kind of resurrection. Once she had made a first tentative sighting of what looked like our man in the Philadelphia record other referential sightings became possible, moving both backward and forward in time.

Through backtracking from the Philadelphia record she dis-covered that my great-grandfather James went first to New York in 1885. He had been a boatman on the river in Carrick. A New York directory of 1885 revealed that he plied the same trade at Pier 1, near Ellis Island (not yet the immigration reception centre, which was still at Castle Garden). He lived in a boarding house at Canal Street. Thomas and Edward Coady boarded nearby. These remain unknown to me: they were probably kin from an earlier migration, since Thomas Coady had been born in America. In the following year, 1886, James married in Philadelphia.

This accorded with a mere wisp of tradition which I had tried to pursue in Carrick. In 1956, while my mother was in hospital, her bed had been beside that of an old woman dying of cancer who told her that the Coadys and Brunnocks (who came from near Carrick) were somehow connected through a marriage in America long ago. The contemporary generation of Brunnocks in and around Carrick were unaware of this. There was one remaining old woman still living in nearby Ballinderry townland who might remember something. Her son Sean Murray arranged for me to meet her, but on the very evening I was to call to her house I was dismayed to discover that she had suddenly taken ill that afternoon and was in a coma. Hannah (Brunnock) Murray died that night, and I stood at her burial on a snowy day under Slievenamon, feeling that the gods were making sport of me.

I had gone back to the basket weaver and the unindexed parish records and laboriously charted and trawled the entire Brunnock genealogy for whatever I might find. I sought a girl of that surname, roughly contemporary with my great-grandfather, who might have emigrated to America. In the church sacristy I had encountered one such possibility through a process of search and elimination. Out of a remark passed thirty years ago to my mother by an old dying woman I had fixed upon the infant Mary Brunnock, baptised in Carrick in 1854, as the woman James Coady could have married after he emigrated. Intuition was straining toward fact in the manner of poet Michael Hartnett's wonderful phrase 'I can foretell the past . . . '

Now independent confirmation came by letter from Eileen McConnell. She had discovered that my great-grandfather James married Mary Brunnock at St Malachy Church, Philadelphia, in June 1886, with Fr Bernard F Gallagher officiating. I was elated. Poetry was anticipating fact. There could be descendants of this marriage still in America. Out of all of this there might be a living person I could find and embrace.

◆§ §◆

The Brunnocks (a residual form of *Breathnach*, usually found in the translated form 'Walsh') were a labouring and boat-hauling family from Ballinderry, a mile upriver from Carrick. Mary had been born there in a thatched cabin beside the river in 1854. She was one of seven children of parents who were Irish speakers. Her older sister Hannah had also emigrated to America in the post-Famine period and was married to a man named Maurice Wall of Philadelphia, where Mary worked as a laundress in a Jewish foster home.

I don't know how or where James Coady and Mary Brunnock met. They had been born in the same river valley, baptised in the same parish font, and possibly knew one another from the Old World before their paths crossed again in the New. They must have married in America with the bright hope of a new beginning. Perhaps James Coady still intended to send for his son Michael in Ireland after he had secured some base of economic and domestic security.

Eileen McConnell sent me a photocopy of the actual Marriage Licence completed in the presence of the couple by an official at the Orphan's Court of Philadelphia and dated 18 June 1886. I recall the tremor in my hands when I unfolded the page to discover my great-grandfather's signature at the foot of the document, like the apparition of a dim figure suddenly glimpsed down a distant corridor.

I have never found a picture of the man and possess no intimation of his living presence, other than that one sign from his shaping hand, a moment on a day of hope when his new life was about to begin with Mary Brunnock, finally reaching me across an ocean and a century.

Obviously he had acquired some basic literacy in America, though he never took out citizenship. Information filed by the official testified that the applicant who stood before him was a widowed labourer born in 1848, and that his former wife had died in Ireland 'some four years since'. Mary Brunnock ('house work') gave her address as Euclid Avenue.

ᑫᏸ ᏸᑐ

Though Philadelphia was still to a large extent the stereotypical city of Quaker traditions, old wealth, conservatism and exclusivity, it was from around 1880 entering the turbulence of an explosive industrialisation that has been called its Iron Age. This rapid expansion of industry and technology threatened to obliterate in a haze of smoke and steam what had been William Penn's 'green country town' of fine squares and green vistas, now increasingly colonised by endless overcrowded clusters of workers' housing, railroads and factories, freight yards and warehouses.

The city was also a premier port of America. James Coady worked around the south Philadelphia waterfront of the Delaware as a casual stevedore and labourer. It was a harsh and brutally competitive world. Waterfront labourers lived at the lowest rung of the Irish-immigrant ladder. Casual stevedores would 'shape up' at street corners close to the wharves every morning, hoping to scramble for a day's work. The eastern cities were expanding rapidly and flooded with Irish and other immigrants, an unlimited and cheap labour pool which was exploited ruthlessly. In 1903 the city experienced its first major strike when 100,000 textile workers demanded a 55-hour week. The strike failed, but it brought to public attention the fact that 10,000 of the striking workers were children, many only ten years old.

The English, Irish and Germans of the 'Old Immigration' were still predominant in the late nineteenth century, but newcomers continually joined the second and third generation Irish of previous migrations. In 1880 the Irish constituted half of the city's foreign-born population of 24%. By 1905 there were 100,000 Jews in the city, 70,000 of them Russian and many of them living in the southern wards. By 1910 there were 70,000 Italians, and Philadelphia also had the largest black population of any northern urban centre. A number of foreign language newspapers were published in the city which had a population of a million-and-a-quarter in 1900.

James and Mary Coady lived in rented rooms: unskilled first-generation immigrants in the cities hardly ever acquired a home of their own. The struggle to survive must have been relentless. South Philadelphia was noted for its poor housing, insanitary conditions and unskilled workers. The slums were not high tenements but narrow alleys and dark courtyards of tiny three-storey houses, one room to the floor, and known as Trinity — 'Father, Son and Holy Ghost'. Endemic political graft frustrated administrative reform at every level.

In *The Irish Relations — Trials of an Immigrant Tradition*, Philadelphia historian Dennis Clark records the struggle of Irish families in urban industrial settings. As late as 1910 the US Immigration Commission investigated several Irish areas in Philadelphia. Almost half of the males were labourers and a quarter of the employed females were domestics. One fifth of the Irish could not read or write. Investigators found the worst kind of slum housing, with outside water supply, outside toilets and open drains. 'With such housing conditions, added to bad working conditions, life for many surely seemed to be a trap . . . '

~❧ ☙~

The Coadys' first child, James, was born in 1888, at 833 Grover Street in the third ward of the city, and baptised at St Philip de Neri Church. A second son, Joseph, was born at the same address in 1890. A third child, Ellen, followed in 1892, by which time the family had moved around the corner to 108 Queen Street. The infant Ellen died at the age of five months, but worse was to follow. On 25 July 1893, at 108 Queen Street, Mary Coady was delivered of a stillborn female infant. On the following day she herself died, aged 39.

James Coady's Oven Lane tragedy had cruelly re-enacted itself in the New World. Both of his wives had died in an agony of childbirth, each after seven years of marriage. By this time in Carrick his son Michael was a youth and working in Bourke's Drapery, but knew nothing of his lost father's whereabouts or predicament.

In Philadelphia James Coady was left with two sons, aged five and three, and the daily struggle for survival. The trail grows less clear. It appears that the children may have been taken in by their aunt, Hannah (Brunnock) Wall, and her husband Maurice. Thereafter James is found boarding mainly with Edward and Elizabeth Ramsey who had been born in Ireland and Scotland respectively. In the Census of 1910, when he was aged 62, he was still boarding, but without his two sons, at the house of Elizabeth Ramsey (by then a widow) at 321 Kimball Street in the parish of St Philip. Also in the house were the American-born nephew and niece of Elizabeth Ramsey, John Hill, 22, ('teamster') and Lizzie Hill, 19, ('soap factory'). All in the house were given as literate.

The 1910 Census records that James Coady had been out of work for twenty weeks in the previous year. In terms of heavy waterfront labour he was already an old man, now twenty-five years living in America and still legally classified as 'Alien'. The Irish by then had moved out of the area and he was surrounded by a new wave of Yiddish-speaking Russian immigrants who mainly worked in the sweatshops of the garment industry.

The remainder of the record is relentlessly stark. In 1911 James Coady's son, James junior (a clerk, 5020 Brown Street) died, aged 22. Four years later, in 1915, his only remaining American-born child, Joseph (an upholsterer, 6615 Lansdowne Avenue), died, aged 25. Both were unmarried, and both died of pulmonary tuberculosis. The informant named on both death certificates was not their father but their maternal uncle through marriage, Maurice Wall, at whose successive addresses they died, and in whose family grave both were buried. At four a.m. on 19 September 1915, six months after the death of his last son, Joseph, James Coady himself died, aged 67, at St Agnes Hospital, Philadelphia. Listed causes of death were a broken hip and 'alcoholic pneumonia'. The funeral was from the boarding house of Elizabeth Ramsey:

> *The Philadelphia Record*, Tuesday Sept 21, 1915
> CODY: [Died] On Sept 19, 1915, JAMES, husband of the late Mary Cody. Relatives and friends of the family, also members of St Philip's Holy Name Society, and American Transport Co. Beneficial Union, are respectfully invited to attend funeral on Wednesday morning at 8.30 o'clock, from the residence of Mrs Elizabeth Ramsey, 321 Kimball St. (3rd and Carpenter Sts.). Solemn High Mass of Requiem at St Philip's Church at 10 o'clock precisely.

My great-grandfather James was buried out at New Cathedral Cemetery on the north side of the city, in a single grave which belonged to a man named Joseph Rice, of whom I know nothing, but who may have donated the grave out of charity or friendship. In the same cemetery the mortal remains of his wife Mary Brunnock Coady and their children rest in the family plot of their cousins the Walls. Why is the father not buried with them? Why had he lived for years in a boarding house and seemingly apart from his two growing sons? That ominous but almost inevitable word *alcoholic* on his death certificate — what anguished family context surrounds it? I can never know. The reason for his burial in a grave apart from his predeceased family may simply be that there was no room remaining in the crowded Wall plot where his son Joseph had been buried only six months before.

When was the single fateful letter to my grandfather Michael in Carrick written? My guess is that it was during the six months in 1915 between the death of Joseph — the last surviving American-born child — and James Coady's own death. Back in Carrick my own father was a boy of nine in that year — old enough to witness and remember for the rest of his life the drama of the letter's arrival and rejection by my grandfather. That first and last letter from Philadelphia must have been the utterance of a broken old man now finally alone and without hope, his conscience returning to the bewildered child he had long ago left in a lane beside the Suir.

❧ ❧

Ireland is often ignorant of the realities of Irish immigrant life in America. We have heard of the trumpeted successes, some of mythically rare proportions, while below those spectacular pinnacles we may be able to guess at an extensive grey middle ground of survival and modest achievement over generations. What remains largely unrecorded is the limbo world of those who sank in failure, the type of wasteland of social disconnection, drift and dereliction memorably recreated and redeemed by William Kennedy in his 'Albany' trilogy and notably *Ironweed*. Stalked by misfortune at every turn of his life, James Coady was trapped at the underbelly of Irish-America at the turn of the century. But out of a poem that seeks to reconcile the dead, and out of the long search by Eileen McConnell, I had repossessed more of his lost story than my father and my deeply wounded grandfather Michael ever knew.

Can words upon the page restore a lost and broken man to the fractured hearthstone of kinship? The father who had abandoned his son was finally himself abandoned. When he reached for pen, paper and words to write his plea for understanding and forgiveness to his son in Ireland long before I was born, it would have been beyond the imagining of this barely literate man that his attempt at articulation would one day lead to the telling of his story at the very heart-centre of American culture and privilege. In March 1989 the singer and actor Liam Clancy included my poem 'The Letter' in a filmed performance at The Poets' Theatre beside Harvard University in Cambridge, Massachusetts.

I knew by now that sooner or later I must visit Philadelphia. Even if there was no living human connection to be encountered there I needed to make a personal pilgrimage; to be on site, to stand and walk in places whose names and associations had emerged out of the dark of time and distance, out of memory and a silence of wounded lives and unreconciled hearts. As a grandson and namesake of the child of Oven Lane I needed to walk the reality of Grover Street, Christian Street, Queen Street, Kimball Street; to look out on the Delaware River; to light a candle at St Malachy Church and at St Philip's; to search out and stand over long forgotten graves in New Cathedral Cemetery. I needed now to reach the son's abandoned father.

II

Philadelphia c. 1895,
a court off an alley near Christian Street

A child is sleeping:
An old man gone.
O, father forsaken,
Forgive your son!
— James Joyce

The woman checking my documents at the US Immigration desk at Shannon asked whether my trip was for business or pleasure. In truth I was travelling on the passport of a poem that crossed frontiers of memory and pain. I was a time traveller, reaching back from Old World present to reconnect with a New World past which I had found, or which had found me. In Carrick on a dark October day of teeming rain in 1990 there had been a knock on the door of the classroom in which I was teaching. The man standing outside in the gloom of the school corridor was stocky in build, with silver hair and a clear, unwavering gaze. *I'm Bernard Croke from Philadelphia.* So obsessed had I become with my search that this statement from a stranger could jolt me, as though confronted by some emissary or revenant. Later that afternoon Bernard and his wife Grace came around to our house, shared a meal, and spoke with me for hours. They had read something I had written of the Oven Lane story, were visiting Ireland and had come to look me up.

We continued long after midnight, my copies of turn of century street maps of the south Philadelphia waterfront — part of the material sent to me by Eileen McConnell — spread out over table and floor. The Crokes and I had immediately established an instinctive rapport, though they must have seen in me a man obsessed.

In the following summer I was on my way to stay with them in Philadelphia and while there to give a poetry reading at St Malachy Church. Early on the morning that I left Carrick in July 1991 I walked through Oven Lane. I was conscious of pilgrimage. The man whose steps I followed had also left in early morning, or so my father thought. The thread of family memory maintained that James Coady had left Oven Lane without waking his sleeping son, perhaps to avoid too anguished a parting. The boy had rubbed the sleep from his eyes to find his father gone. This in itself would salt the lifelong wound. The father had left without saying goodbye.

The poem which began out of a suppressed and half-forgotten story had taken on a life of its own, causing things to happen, bringing me now to walk in ritual replay through Oven Lane before I travel on to Shannon and step on board an Aer Lingus 747. The woman at Immigration stamps my documents, looks up with a smile and wishes me a happy holiday in the United States. But for the ghosts in my head and in my blood I set off alone.

My last visit to America was in 1982, before the Oven Lane memory had ripened to resurface in my head. My journeys out of Ireland are rare enough for me to wonder still at transatlantic flight, to marvel at the fact of sitting in the air miles above the Atlantic while being catapulted westwards with hundreds of other people as I sip a glass of wine and scribble in my notebook. A young woman beside me on the plane pointedly avoids conversation until we are more than halfway through our journey, then suddenly opens up. She's Irish but has lived in New York City for some years. Returning there now after six months at home with her mother. Back to New York to complete her Master's in Family Therapy. A demanding occupation? Stressful, yes: New York family therapists are regularly required to undergo mandatory therapy to protect them from collateral damage inherent in being therapists. No hint of irony in her tone and I don't dare risk a sardonic eyebrow. After all, my own journey is about some kind of healing.

In my notebook I've scribbled the simple phrase *Going to America* and suddenly feel the weight of it and the gulf between what it means now and what it must have meant last century. America is a place I know about, like everyone of my time. Even before being there I've constantly heard its speech, known its rhythms, felt its energies, fed on its images. America has projected itself back into the Old World; it has endlessly unreeled itself in every little town and now asserts itself each day in every living room. To enter the place itself is for us now to enter the familiar, even if subtly and essentially foreign on deeper encounter. What image however could the word *America* evoke for the Oven Lane boatman as he set out in 1885? Or for the boy who woke to find his father gone there? The man had never before crossed a sea, never seen a transatlantic liner, never entered a great city, never read a book. In the Oven Lane of more than a century ago *America* must have meant some kind of mythical place; a construct of the imagination, built upon fragmented reports relayed in emigrants' letters or the lore of the occasional exiles who made it back again to the homeland.

James Coady reached New York harbour after a voyage of a week or more in steerage. The Statue of Liberty was not yet finished. He was processed through Castle Garden before he entered into a teeming and tumultuous city which still had its immigrant shanty towns but where Irish labourers and contractors had recently earned themselves the status of having built Brooklyn Bridge, begun in 1869 but not finished until 1883 and hailed as 'the eighth wonder of the world'. The man who faced into this overwhelming metropolis was no longer young, but a widower of thirty-seven who had buried two young children and a wife and left a boy of eight behind him in Ireland. He probably possessed little more than the clothes he wore, the boots in which he stood.

❧ ❦

His New World arrival and my own could not be more different. Though I too have hardly any urban skills, my brief contact with New York after we land causes me no trauma. Bernard Croke has made a booking for me with 'Dave's Limo', a minibus service to Philadelphia which is about two and a half hours away. I dial a number and am told where to wait for my transport just outside the airport arrival building. To my relief the heat is not as intense as had been forecast, and the New York sky is overcast. Though I have never been inside this city it carries passionate resonances for me: since my early teens I have been a lover of jazz, and deeply engaged with all its rich mythologies. I know about the great bands and the classic solos and the sessions, the sidemen and their nicknames, the wild lives and the litanies of place and time that tell the history of this music's urgent joy, its sensual tenderness and blazing affirmation. Some other time I'll enter New York City for its jazz; my mission now will focus on a time before the quintessential American art form had been conceived and born in New Orleans, brought up the Mississippi and gone out to evangelise the world.

Refreshing rain comes swirling across the highway and its unbroken lanes of traffic during my journey to Philadelphia. I share the trip with an exhausted old woman returning from Warsaw. She has been in America since she was fourteen, looks like an Irish countrywoman, but speaks English, Polish, Lithuanian and German. She has been back in eastern Europe to see her relatives — for the last time, she says with tears. She's too old for the journey now and will never leave Philadelphia again. She is puzzled when I speak of Ireland and can't locate it in the maps in her old head.

We cross the Delaware, and my sense of pilgrimage heightens. On the waterfront of this great river the boatman from the Suir toiled more than a century ago. The old woman who has been to Warsaw is dropped off, speaking a blessing to me as she goes. I am carried to a leafy neighbourhood in north-east Philadelphia and right to the door of my hosts. In honour of my arrival the Crokes have hung out the Irish tricolour beside the Stars and Stripes. Bernard and Grace are both American-born, but deeply immersed in Irish-American cultural life and voluntary enterprises. Their telephone rings constantly and their home often functions as a kind of unofficial consulate.

The rain has cleared and the sudden dusk of north America falls while we talk and share food and drinks under trees in the garden until near to midnight. I am blessed to have found such hosts, blessed that they should have found their way to me. Upstairs my room is ready. Though it is only hours since I walked through Oven Lane, the journey I have come here to complete began when Walt Whitman was living out his last years across the Delaware in Camden, and Charles Stewart Parnell was still Ireland's uncrowned king.

✒ ✒

One of the ironies of James Coady's story is that of his two marriages and two families the only child who survived to marry and have descendants was his abandoned son Michael in Ireland. From him derive all my relatives in the paternal line, including American cousins from a later migration by my uncle Jimmy, who left Carrick permanently in 1920. His daughter Mae Coady Jones arrives from Connecticut to join me in Philadelphia. She too is a great-grandchild of the boatman of Oven Lane and has learned his hidden story from me. In brilliant sunshine we travel by

Roosevelt Boulevard and Rising Sun Avenue towards New Cathedral Cemetery, now in an industrial area with miles of urban development around and beyond it, but originally at the green northern edge of the city. We find the curator's office at Butler Street, and meet with Sean Feeley, who is from Mayo, but has worked at this job for twenty years.

Shelved in an annexe are bound volumes recording thousands of burials since 1860, each grave identified by section, range and plot. New Cathedral is not among the largest of Philadelphia's cemeteries, but to my small town eye it is a vast settlement of subterranean memory, a place of silenced multitudes.

And so through streets and intersections of the dead I am finally led to Section Y, Range 7, Lot 25: the single grave of James Coady, still registered as the property of Joseph Rice, whoever he may have been. As I expected, there is no headstone or memorial marker. After the American fashion the whole area is lawned, with many trees, but Sean Feeley measures out the space exactly. There are few headstones in this section, and close by is the corner of the cemetery once set apart for unbaptised infants. Near my great-grandfather's grave is a mature cherry tree.

Eternal greetings to the dead. This is where the boatman's journey from Oven Lane in 1885 ended in 1915. I have travelled across an ocean, and through three generations, to stand over this unmarked patch of grass. Has anyone come to visit here since the handful of mourners turned away after the burial on Wednesday, 22 September 1915? What can I do to mark this moment, now that I finally stand here above the grave's proverbial silence? What else but sidestep reason into ancient invocation? *Our Father, who art in heaven . . .*

The date of James Coady's death and the place of his burial had long eluded Eileen McConnell even after all else that could be retrieved of the story had already been uncovered. When no record of his death was forthcoming Eileen and her husband Ken had travelled to Philadelphia from Maryland to search the relevant public records in person, only to learn that, through a bureaucratic quirk or oversight, they were not there and might be lodged in a repository in Pittsburgh. Similarly, though the record of the other Coady burials in New Cathedral Cemetery had been found, James Coady's own grave had still eluded recognition in the indexes because his burial was recorded under the primary heading of the registered owner of the plot, Joseph Rice.

In 1989 I was spending a summer in Newfoundland and had just returned to the home of my hosts John and Maura Mannion in St John's after a stay on the remote island of Fogo. I was still sleeping on the morning after the long journey back from that island when I was roused to take a telephone call from Washington. It was Eileen McConnell. After months of searching she had finally located the date and place of James Coady's death and the site of his single grave. Prior to this we had been exploring various hypotheses, including the possibility that he might have spent the last part of his life in some institution. During that period of trying to guess at the likely circumstances of James's death I had come across and written into my journal a sentence of Rilke: *Each man bears his own death within himself*. Now the final parameter of the narrative fell into place like a gate clanging shut: he had died in September 1915 when he was still boarding with Elizabeth Ramsey at Kimball Street, six months after the death of his last American-born son, Joseph.

It was strange to be standing in Newfoundland, receiving this news of a family death over the phone from Washington. 'How did he die?' I asked Eileen. 'The death certificate says alcoholic pneumonia and a broken hip,' she told me. As though a button had been pressed, my imagination instantly 'foretold' the past in flashback: a man too old for waterfront work staggering and falling in an alleyway at night and lying there unheeded until morning.

That evening I was meeting with the poet Harold Paddock who lives in St John's at Carrick Street — named after my own town. In a downtown bar we ran into Mary Dalton, another poet, and the night became a kind of surrogate wake for James Coady as I told of the news I had heard and the story behind it. The place was *Talamh an Éisc* and the date August 1989 but the death in Philadelphia felt close and real, as if contemporaneous with that morning's message rather than seventy-four years back in real time.

And forgive us our trespasses, as we forgive those who trespass against us. In New Cathedral Cemetery the sun beats down and birds are singing. Immediately beyond the boundary fence the urgent life of late twentieth-century America throbs palpably. All this area had once been part of the extensive eighteenth-century plantation of John Michael Browne who was born in County Galway and studied medicine in France before emigrating to the West Indies and then to America. Dr Browne, a wealthy Catholic, endowed chapels and owned slaves. Among its many provisions his Last Will and Testament bequeathed to his sister, Anastasia Dillon, 'two Negroes valued at £30 and £35; a woman, Hannah, and a boy, Tom'. Browne's wish was to be buried in part of the orchard on his plantation and to allow his neighbours the same privilege afterwards. Out of this grew New Cathedral Cemetery, with the city soon expanding all around and miles beyond it. At night now the gates are locked and guard dogs released in the grounds to protect the resting places of the dead from molestation by the living.

Before I leave Philadelphia at the end of my three week visit I will return here repeatedly and sit under the tree beside James Coady's grave. The few gravestones in this section all carry Irish names, as do most of the stones throughout the cemetery: Duffy, Nolan, Murphy, McGovern, Carroll, Keenan, McNamara, Donnelly, Dougherty, Clancy. The boatman of Oven Lane, or his unforgiving son, or that child's son in turn who was my father, could not have imagined my coming here.

We search out the grave in another section of the cemetery where Mary Brunnock Coady and her three children lie with their cousins, the Walls — related through Mary's sister, Hannah Brunnock Wall. Two women from Ballinderry, beside the Suir. This grave too is unmarked. My imagination replays known instances of human grief enacted over this mute patch of grass a century ago: the young mother dead in childbirth; the infant daughter gone the year before; the two remaining sons who would follow in their twenties. James Coady stood at this graveside to see infant, wife and sons buried successively between 1892 and 1915, until with his last son Joseph's burial he was finally alone, and with six months left to live. Today the grass is decked with flowering clover. Between the trees the sun beats down from the relentless blue.

On my first Sunday in the city Bernard and Grace drive me to Mass in one of the southern wards. The parish of St Philip de Neri is the principal locale of my great-grandfather's story: this is the river ward in which the Coady family lived and died in poor and overcrowded conditions. The Italianate church itself was built in 1841. It was besieged during violent anti-Irish-Catholic riots in Philadelphia in 1844, the worst such riots in American history, necessitating the deployment on the streets of 5,000 troops to stop loss of life and the torching of homes, churches and convents. At St Philip's in 1847 a memorial sermon in Irish was preached after the death of Daniel O'Connell.

Here the children of James Coady's Philadelphia marriage were baptised, here the family went to church, and here the mother and father's Requiem Masses were finally offered in 1893 and 1915 respectively. The resident parishioners have now dwindled to a couple of hundred old people, with young professional couples resettling the neighbourhood and inflating rents and property prices. They don't go to church, these new young people, the old parish priest Fr Sikora later tells me. Their lives don't need communion or baptisms or Masses. They don't have babies; they have careers. The parish may be in terminal decline and the accountants of the Archdiocese may eventually decide to close the church notwithstanding its historical and architectural distinction.

On our way in to midday Mass the sun is blazing and the air heavy and humid. Since the number of active parishioners declined most services are now held not in the main church that is stepped up above the street but in a smaller basement chapel through an entrance suggestive of a crypt. I am deeply moved to be here, a century after James Coady and his wife Mary, and I light candles for them and their children before the ceremony begins. Nothing prepares my already heightened imagination for what dramatically explodes out of the blue during the Mass — the church suddenly darkening, wind through the wide open windows whirling and scattering prayer leaflets, the cosmic flare and crackle of lightning, the shattering detonation of thunder and cloudburst even as the priest raises the chalice. In my suggestible state I am shaken by it, as by some kind of dramatic pentecostal visitation, and so, I think, are the Crokes.

This sudden brief storm takes the whole city by surprise, and leaves tree damage, surface flooding and power disruption. Back in the Crokes' garden it has overturned chairs and split a quince tree in two. Thereafter we jokingly refer to this cosmic outburst on my first visit to St Philip's as 'the Coady storm'. For me the joke has a slightly unnerving edge. I have brought with me from Ireland a file of papers and references relating to my search. The sudden violent wind through the open window has scattered the papers all over my upstairs room. The journal that I keep has been blown open on the desk beside the window. The page is wet and the words I wrote last night have blurred and run together. *Sunt lacrimae rerum et mentem mortalia tangunt.* These are tears of things and touch all mortal minds.

Robert Emmet Brennan is newly appointed to assist in St Philip's parish. In the post-Famine period some of his Irish immigrant ancestors worked under conditions of near-slavery in the coalmines of upstate Pennsylvania. Fr Brennan has taught literature for twenty-five years before being seconded to St Philip's, and he reads my poem and its associated narrative with deep interest.

When I request that a Mass be said for the Coady family who lived and died in this parish a century ago he responds enthusiastically. He offers early Mass each morning for a week, announcing the intention publicly on each occasion, and including the family in Ireland, both living and dead. On the first and last of these mornings Bernard and I are spruced up, through the early morning traffic and downtown at the church by 7.30, even if we have been sitting in the garden sharing beers and talk into the small hours. I participate in the readings and for the last of the week's Masses we are joined by Grace, just home from her night shift as a nurse.

I remember it as a beautiful morning, full of some unmistakable sense of benediction, with sunshine sidelighting and defining old cobblestones and trolley-car tracks close to the waterfront. After we left the church we walked about the waking streets and bought fresh bread in a small Jewish bakery. An effulgent and voluptuous image stays with me. An *aisling*. I recall a tall and backlit girl in a flowing white dress striding along on the opposite side of the street. Coming towards us out of the morning light, and passing on. She walked with the energised grace of a trained dancer; the essence of vibrant life and beauty in a woman. Who was she? What was her story? Where was she coming from? Where was she going? Why do I remember her?

On that radiant morning close to the waterfront I felt unmistakably blessed beyond reason and I sensed that Bernard and Grace were bathed in it too, though nothing was explicitly said. From our first meeting I had recognised the strength of their bond, the jokey ease and interplay of a love securely rooted. Moments of happiness and epiphany may only be fully recognised in retrospect and in the shadow of loss. As the three of us together walked the streets that morning we could not suspect that Bernard would be dead in a year.

Other days are given to searching out the network of street addresses at which the Coadys lived from 1886 to 1915 in St Philip de Neri parish. Eileen McConnell's research has been meticulous; I have with me copies from the National Archives in Washington of contemporary Philadelphia street maps of the area pinpointing exactly where the Coadys lived.

This waterfront district is not far from the historic heart of the Founding Fathers' Philadelphia or from its modern high-rise centre. In my great-grandfather's time it was a teeming warren of immigrants set against a constantly shifting urban mosaic of competing ethnic groups. Blacks had been migrating north to Philadelphia since the Civil War. Successive waves of impoverished Irish were followed by East-European Jews and Italians. The row houses were small brick dwellings, sweat-boxes in summer and freezing in winter, lining narrow streets, overcrowded alleys and courts. Urban America almost by definition constantly tears down and rebuilds; I am fortunate to find the area I have come to see still relatively intact. The neighbourhood has now become fashionable, with upwardly-mobile couples restoring the houses in what is an intimate neighbourhood. In my great-grandfather's time Irish and other immigrant families struggled to pay rent, find work, and raise children in slum conditions of open drains and contaminated water supply. In 1906 the annual rate of deaths from typhoid in the city rose to 1,063. The City Health Department put up scare posters (*Prevent the Plague!*) and paid a bounty of five cents for every live rat captured and delivered to the Rat Depot.

All of the successive addresses I find are in an area as compact as that between Carrick's Main Street and the river Suir, with the same pattern of street cluster fronted by a river, the configuration differing only in scale. When I stand in the sunshine at the threshold of the little house on the corner at 108 Queen Street I can only stare dumbly at its weathered stone doorstep, reflecting on lives that crossed it. It was here the Coadys' third child Ellen was born in 1892 and died after five months, and here also in the following year Mary died on a stillbirth, aged 39, after twenty-four hours in labour. Her husband was widowed for the second time, while still scrambling for work on the waterfront, and with two boys aged three and five to care for. The year of Mary's death also saw the beginning of an economic depression that would last through the decade.

I agonise there at the door of 108 Queen Street. Should I ring the bell and try to explain who I am and what brings me here to whoever lives there now? Would they want to know about the old burden of Irish memory that I carry back to their theshold? In the end I can't find the nerve to press the doorbell. There is too much to explain at that door, most of it an emotion beyond articulation. Can a house hold something of the lives that have been lived within it, that something suggested in John Montague's phrase, 'absent presence'? My great-grandfather was one insignificant pebble on a vast shore. Though his life was one of failure and tragedy it must have been relieved by human interludes of joy and laughter, along with the brief escape dispensed in gin-mill and saloon.

Close by I stand on the waterfront and look across the Delaware River, about a mile wide at this point. Across in Camden, on the New Jersey shore, Walt Whitman lies buried. Steam had not yet completely ousted sail when the boatman of Oven Lane bent and sweated here. Philadelphia was among the busiest ports of the United States. City ferries plied constantly with New Jersey and the first bridge spanning the Delaware would not be built until the 1920s. This waterfront was a teeming and turbulent arena of arrival and departure, transaction and toil for generations. The world is built out of the sweat of the forgotten, that invisible host saluted in Bob Dylan's 'Song to Woody':

Here's to the hearts and the hands of the men
That came with the dust and are gone with the wind.

Years of mornings, light and dark and in all weathers, James
Coady walked here to the 'shape up' at the corner of Christian
Street where I stand in the sunshine a hundred years on. Here he
stood and offered himself for heavy, dangerous and irregular
work, with unlimited hours, and at a bare subsistence wage. The
strength of a man's back was all he had to sell. Gangs of workers,
black or Irish, competed to outpace and undercut each other in
loading or unloading ships from rat-infested piers and wharves or
offshore tenders.

In the half-mile stretch of waterfront near where James lived
were berths for ferries serving Atlantic City, Gloucester and
Kaighns Point in New Jersey, along with thirty or more crowded
wharves and warehouses for freight and larger piers to serve the
Pennsylvania & Reading Railroad, the Allen Line for Glasgow
and Liverpool, the Hamburg American Line, the Atlantic Trans-
port Line, the American Line and the Red Star Line for Antwerp.
Dockers' attempts to organise invariably met with police brutal-
ity, company strike-breakers, violence, intimidation and black-
listing against a background of political corruption and ruthless
exploitation. Fatal or crippling accidents were common and could
condemn a family to destitution. Men aged early. Wives took in
washing or sewing; children could work long hours in stifling
textile mills and never know a childhood.

A high human price was paid for America's phenomenal
industrial expansion, development and wealth. In 1878 the
Philadelphia Public Ledger published this statement of an Irish
mother in response to concerted allegations that the poor
neglected their children:

> It is very true that the woman who makes seersucker coats for
> six cents apiece or does other sewing at the same rate, and has to
> work eighteen hours out of the twenty-four cannot spare a
> minute to take care of her child, and all the time she takes to
> wash, dress and feed it is so much time stolen from the effort to
> keep a roof over its head or get it bread.

Jerry Kelly is an old-timer with long roots among the waterfront Irish of south Philadelphia. It is possible and even likely, he tells me, that my great-grandfather worked for his, George Kelly, a man who married four wives and was the organiser of gangs of Irish dockers who were hired on the corner of South and Christian streets, or that he may have worked for one of that patriarch's flamboyant sons, among them George the Harp, Charlie the Devil, Billy the Chief, Fran the Handsome . . .

A time traveller from the future, I walk along South Front Street, my slanted shadow moving ahead of me to find house number 830. It carries a 'For Sale' sign. In 1900, when he was seven years a widower for the second time but seemingly without his two young sons, James boarded briefly at this location and the list of other residents was probably typical of the demographic character of the area at the turn of the century. The head of the house was Philip Carroll (53), with his sisters Bridget (40) and Margaret (38) and boarders Mickel O'Brien, senior (52), James Day (32), Mickel O'Brien, junior (21), Patrick Kelly (52), Mickel Cuningham (30) and Murty Kelly (26). The 1900 Census shows that all but Mickel O'Brien junior were Irish-born and had variously emigrated to America between 1866 and 1885. With the exception of the widowed Mickel O'Brien senior and the twice-widowed James Coady all were single. The two women were housekeepers and all but one of the men stevedores.

These were raw and transient waterfront communities, still too close to a subsistence struggle to be able to formulate any lace-curtain ambitions. Their play must have been as rough as their work and their living conditions. Hard drinking was endemic, and the saloon a centre for contact, negotiation, political organisation and swapping of news and information. The brash vernacular culture into which they entered was a bubbling and indiscriminate stew of the ethnic and the crudely commercial. Elements of their older culture endured almost by default, with commercial tunesmiths also providing vaudeville songs of nostalgia and stage-Irishness. Such commercial ditties sometimes attempted to bridge the ethnic market with songs like that extolling the charms of *Nelly O'Morgan with her barrel organ, the Irish-Italian girl*. A more daring ethnic alliance was suggested in *My Yiddisher Colleen* . . .

One element of Irish-American community could bridge and

transcend all the change and dislocation between homeland and New World. Most of the immigrant Irish brought with them not only some pre-Christian sense of otherworld buried deep in their psyche, but also membership of a vast multinational organisation: the Roman Catholic Church. Within its New World matrix they found and formed familiar structures of parish and all its rituals of worship and belonging. Their unstable neighbourhoods struggled to define themselves around parish church and school, with the milestones of individual and family lives marked and dignified in sacramental rites of birth, marriage and death. Whether they survived or sank in the maelstrom of material struggle and however tenuous or tattered their individual faith and practice might become, once they stepped inside the church porch and dipped fingers in the holy water font to bless themselves they entered a space where all mundane perspective was subverted. Here all that happened or might happen in their lives could be subsumed and sanctified within a well of meaning and eternal purpose. Here they ranked not as longshoremen or labourers, harassed factory hands or housekeepers, but, in the last analysis, individual and immortal souls.

Whatever the sorrows, degradations and humiliations of James Coady's broken life, over his coffin at the last a Mass of Requiem was chanted, its solemn cadences transcending the tired usage of the priest or the impatience of the pews, with incense and invocation rising out of all and over all: *Agnus Dei, qui tollis peccata mundi, dona eis requiem sempiternam.* When I come searching in Philadelphia one hundred years on it is primarily to churches I must go for a sense of communing contact with the spirits of those I seek, just as, in the homeland, it was in the sacristy unlocked for me by the basket weaver that I principally found their presences encoded.

❧☙

Of his thirty years in America James Coady knew only seven of married family life. All the addresses at which he lived both as husband and widower were clustered near waterfront and 'shape up'. The narrow streets of the district typically held small row houses, blind alley courts, ramshackle wooden warrens serving as boarding houses for single men ('walk to work housing'), gin-mills, warehouses and supply lofts for shipping. Though only a mile from City Hall, the area's teeming squalor and boisterous life were a world removed from the patrician Philadelphia of immense wealth, stately homes and Quaker origins. The private trains and yachts, the winter castles and summer 'cottages' of the Philadelphia rich equalled those of their New York counterparts, even if less flaunted, being Philadelphian. At exclusive Assembly balls new-rich aspirants danced and sought alliances with well-bred Peppers, Newbolds, Biddles and Cadwaladers, while well below such social peaks a large middle class of many gradations aspired towards respectability and conformity. If this conservative city neglected its own great painter Thomas Eakins in his lifetime, it nevertheless directed considerable riches to philanthropic ends and public patronage. One of its great institutions, dating from 1891, is the Free Library of Philadelphia. I spend hours in its downtown main branch, reeling time backwards through old newspapers, opening windows on the quotidian past.

What is happening in the city on Friday, 18 June 1886, when James Coady and Mary Brunnock set off to marry at St Malachy's? The drivers of the city's horse-drawn street cars are demanding a weekly wage of $10 with a reduction of their working day from fifteen to twelve hours. Four hundred city grave-diggers seek better conditions and no work on the Sabbath except in the case of infectious diseases. There are reports of people hospitalised due to heat prostration. Striking upstate coalminers convicted of conspiracy begin their eight month jail sentences, with a petition for their pardon being circulated by the Knights of Labor. Fairmount Steamers advertise an evening cruise on the Schuylkill River with 33 Celebrated Musicians. There are boxing challenges announced, combined with minstrel shows. The Mayor has requested the police to flush the gutters of the city at least once a day during July and August. A correspondent compares a Democratic ward boss to a rattlesnake. There is news of a negro lynching in Nebraska and riots in Belfast, Ireland. A Jersey City man is said to have sold his wife to a Hoboken blacksmith for $20. A woman who had been suffering from Nervous and Prostrated Feelings, Wind, Headache, Dizziness, Heaviness, Dull, Languid and Prostrated Spells testifies that she has passed a Tape Worm 63 feet long as a result of taking Dr E. F. Kunkel's Unique Internal Remedy. J. J. Dillon announces the opening of a First Class Drinking Saloon at S.E. corner 9th Street and Girard Avenue, and Professor F. C. Fowler offers a Valuable Treatise (sealed) to Weak Men suffering from the effects of Youthful Errors. In the employment columns an amateur circus seeks 25 Young Men 'that can passably ride a horse' for two weeks at a shore in August, while there is an opening at 716 N. 36th Street for 'A Half-Grown Girl to assist in General Housework'.

America was already mythologising and marketing itself. On that summer day of James and Mary's wedding a Magnificent Cyclorama of the Battle of Gettysburg is open for viewing at the corner of North Broad and Cherry, but the greatest spectacle in town, and in its second week, is one directed by a Cody: *America's National Entertainment* — Buffalo Bill's Wild West Show — *More General Features of Western Life Than Ever Before at One Time and Place Visible on the Face of the Globe*. It was exactly ten years since Chief Sitting Bull, who toured with the show, had led the Sioux at the massacre of General Custer's troops at Little Bighorn after the government had broken its resettlement treaty with his people.

❧ ❧

To my complete surprise my wife Martina arrives from Ireland. She's here to be with me for a special occasion, and the hurried conspiracy that has enabled her to fly to America and leave the children in good hands has involved the kindness and inspiration of friends on both sides of the ocean. There are times when all things fall together in a providential harmony.

The occasion is the public reading which I am giving at St Malachy Church on a Sunday which also happens to be our wedding anniversary. The reading is organised jointly by the Irish American Cultural Institute and the parish, with Bernard Croke the essential mover behind it. Before my arrival in Philadelphia invitations have gone out bearing reproductions of a print made for the occasion by the artist Robert McGovern along with my Oven Lane poem. St Malachy's is a beautiful church originally built by Irish immigrants in the 1850s in an area now become a social wasteland in the north of the city.

This is the parish in which Mary Brunnock lived and worked until she married James Coady and moved south to the waterfront wards with him. Again I am blessed by circumstance. The pastor at St Malachy's is John McNamee, a poet and writer whose parents were Irish-born. The rectory in which he lives as parish priest frequently functions as an oasis of sanctuary for people in trouble or crisis. With a few religious sisters and other helpers he ministers heroically on the harrowing frontier of urban America's appalling and intractable problems — drugs and crime, alcoholism, poverty, family breakdown and social chaos.

At Sunday morning's Mass in this opulently appointed church, first built by the post-Famine Irish, the choir and small local congregation are mainly black, the attendance complemented by friends and supporters of St Malachy's and its adjacent school who faithfully gather to worship here on Sunday from other parts of the city and suburbs. From the day's gospel John McNamee talks about healing, relating it to the current human story of his broken community, welcoming my wife and me and telling the reason for our presence. A Muslim man released after fourteen years in prison on a questionable conviction goes to the pulpit and thanks the priest and people for their successful appeal on his behalf. The sung prayers from the black cantor include the names of my great-grandfather and his wife Mary. Before the final blessing my wife and I are invited to the altar and given flowers for our anniversary to the applause of the congregation.

My reading in the church is at five o'clock on the same after-noon, with harpist Sinéad Ní hArgadáin and flautist Linda Thomas. The audience includes Eileen and Ken McConnell, who have travelled from Maryland; the artist Robert McGovern; my cousin Mae Coady Jones and her husband Bob from Connecticut; the historian Dennis Clark whose books on the Irish immigrant experience have opened up realities of that world to me. Here too is Michael Doyle, the priest, community leader and anti-war activist of Sacred Heart parish in Camden, a vital centre of hope and renewal in the midst of devastation. There are also members of the arts and academic community, among them the poet Joseph Meredith and the fabled librarian and now lamented Michael Durkan.

For me to speak in this place is a privilege and mystery in which past and present fuse around location and the word. I stand on the altar steps before which James Coady and Mary Brunnock stood to be married on a June day in 1886, with Mary McCarthy and

William Torpey as their witnesses. Here the man and woman stood in hope together, untouched by premonition of the pain that lay before them in their lives and would darkly reach beyond them into mine, across an ocean, across a century. On this given day I am come from the future, the grandson and namesake of the abandoned child of Oven Lane, a single lighted candle by my side, the pathos of their lives an open book before me as I begin with words of Keats: *I am certain of nothing but the holiness of the heart's affections and the truth of imagination.*

I leave the Oven Lane poem until last. Before I reach it the harpist sings a setting of Yeats's *Had I the heavens' embroidered cloths.* And so the moment comes for me to voice the lines which have led me to America and to here. Once again I meet with coincidence, an intense and unscripted intervention. I am more than halfway through the poem when the bell begins to toll above the church. It is the six o'clock Angelus, measuring itself out gravely through the poem's cadences and accompanying me precisely to the close:

> *I send this telling out*
> *to meet the ghosts of its begetting;*
> *to release it from stone mouths*
> *of Oven Lane.*

The unforseen congruence of poem and tolling bell affects the audience and leaves me trembling.

Scores of people cram into the rectory for food and drinks and talk. Everyone has a story to tell me of family or of Ireland and America, and some are still deep in discussion with me two hours later when the Crokes spirit me away and back to the house for a more private celebration. This day in my life has been given like a grace.

&ᴄ ᴈᴅ

James Coady spent the last ten years of his life in the small lodging house kept by the Scottish-born widow Elizabeth Ramsey at 321 Kimball Street. This section of street is the only location I search for which has been obliterated. In its place now is a high-rise public housing 'project' into which I am advised not to risk venturing. Elizabeth Ramsey would have known more of the story of James Coady than anyone else. His funeral was from her little lodging house and she was the informant on his death certificate. Before that she saw his struggle to find work as he aged, the deaths of his two sons in their early twenties, and the alcoholism, injury and pneumonia which led to his death at sixty-seven.

There must have been many times when he could not pay for his keep and survived on her charity. I can only guess at the circumstances in which he sat down in that house in Kimball Street to write his single letter to his son Michael in Carrick in the last months of his life. The Yiddish-speaking families surrounding him now were, according to the 1910 Census, all out of Russia: Lazarwitch, Steinberg, Greenwald, Rothman, Schwartz . . . Having lost all in America, perhaps James had some desperate hope that he might return to end his days in Ireland. Though he died abandoned and unanswered he had lit a candle for the future. If he had not struggled with pen and page there could never have been my father's boyhood memory of the letter's dramatic arrival and burning in Carrick, there could never have been my poem or my journey to Philadelphia. The pen in his semi-literate hand foreshadowed the pen in mine, three generations on.

At City Hall I discovered a probate document compiled a month after my great-grandfather's death. Elizabeth Ramsey petitioned as a creditor and was granted James Coady's 'estate' of $110, in the absence of a will.

If this meant actual cash he held at the time of his death my belief is that she would have had ready access to it in lieu of debt without formal process. The declared 'estate' of $110 is likely to have been a death or burial benefit payable by the American Transport Co Beneficial Union. Elizabeth died in her eighties in 1932. The last decade of her life overlapped the presence in America of my future father and two uncles as young immigrants in New York, Long Island and Hartford, but they knew nothing of her, or of the Philadelphia story she could tell about their father's lost father. I pay my respects at her grave in New Cathedral Cemetery, certain that, whatever the exact nature of their relationship, she sheltered James in his last years, and knew his darkest hours.

The closest I had hitherto been able to come to my great-grand-father's physical reality is his signature on the marriage licence issued to him and Mary Brunnock on their wedding day. There emerges a macabre addition to that fragment. The undertaking business of Anthony K Murphy was long established among the Irish communities of south Philadelphia and it was this firm which carried out my great-grandfather's burial. When Bernard Croke and I go looking I am amazed to discover that the under-taking business still exists in its original location, though recently taken over as the Murphy Ruffenach Funeral Home. The new owner Michael Ruffenach is sympathetic to my search. Out of mounds of dusty papers in the basement the detailed bill for the stevedore's funeral in 1915 miraculously surfaces seventy-six years on. The itemised account evokes the ironic and macabre experience of intimate encounter with his corpse:

Interment:
James Coady, 321 Kimball St.   September 22, 1915

Square end chestnut Casket:	$75.00
Chestnut case:	25.00
Hearse to New Cathedral:	7.00
Three carriages — one extra to W. Philadelphia:	19.50
Pall bearers' bus:	7.00
Embalming body:	10.00
Advertising:	6.00
Suit of Clothes:	12.00
Dressing:	3.00
Undergarments:	1.50
Candles & Gloves:	4.00
Shaving & Slippers:	2.50
Blanket & Handkerchief:	5.50
Permit & Affidavits:	1.75
Church Services:	25.00
Flowers:	5.00
Opening Grave:	7.50

The extra carriage to West Philadelphia was, I can guess, for the family of Maurice Wall. The funeral bill amounting to $217.25 was marked paid, probably by Elizabeth Ramsey and with the likely assistance of the longshoremen's union or the parish of St Philip Holy Name Society of which James was a member.

On the Wednesday morning that the small cortège assembled at Elizabeth Ramsey's that day's *Philadelphia Record* was reporting the war in Europe under the heading 'Guns Hit Teutons Hard'. A long propaganda piece urged immigrants to discard any 'foreign allegiance' and not to be 'hyphenated Americans', with a cartoon Irishman declaring: 'I've no use for a hyphen unless that's what ye call the little jigger between the O and the Grady in me name!' A boy was in a critical condition in hospital after drinking a quart of whiskey. The wife of Owen Tracey was suing for divorce on the grounds that her husband had not bathed for twenty-six years and preferred to stay in the cellar, and Mr & Mrs Charles J. Rhoads of South Rittenhouse Square had returned from a month's trip through the Northwest and Canadian Rockies. There were 'Hot Judgeship Fights in Several Counties' and John D. Rockefeller Jnr was attempting to quell a 'labor war' in Colorado through personal intervention: 'Bed in Mining Camp is Rockefeller's Rest — Swings Pick in His Own Mine and Dines with Workmen in Cook Shack!' The many burlesque and vaudeville shows available in the city were now sometimes supplemented by silent movie presentations. Sophie Tucker, 'The Original Singer of Syncopated Melodies', was sharing the bill at the Chestnut Street Theatre with Gertrude Hoffman, 'The Beautiful Slave of Fatal Enchantment', in a variety programme which included Charles Mack & Co. in 'A Natural Irish Comedy'. At the Walnut Theatre straight melodrama was represented by Richard Buhler, 'Famous Hero of Ben Hur', and Company in *The Sign of the Cross*. Al White's New Dance Palace had engaged Kerr's Invincible Dance Orchestra 'of picked men' and warned that it permitted No Freak Dancing.

In its fourth week at the Forrest Theatre was *The Birth of a Nation*, the four column spread trumpeting its $500,000 cost, 5,000 scenes, 3,000 horses, and 18,000 people, the showing enhanced by a synchronised score performed by a 40-piece live orchestra: 'Most Stupendous Dramatic Spectacle the Brain of Man Has Yet Envisioned and Revealed — It Will Make a Better

American of You!' Philadelphia negroes thought otherwise; a delegation was attempting to meet Mayor Blankenburg following the clubbing by police on the preceding Monday evening of a large number of negroes who had been protesting outside the theatre about Griffith's depiction of their race in the movie.

There would be a long deferred but poignant Carrick epilogue to the little funeral wending its way northwards through the city from St Philip's to New Cathedral Cemetery after the Requiem Mass on the morning of Wednesday, 22 September 1915. I was told of it by Kathy Coady, widow of my uncle Peter, when she was in her eighties. She was particularly fond of my grandfather Michael, her father-in-law, and he often confided in her. To the very end of her days Kathy's regard for him left her unbending in condemnation of the father who had abandoned him as an orphaned child, notwithstanding any of the stark facts I had uncovered of James Coady's life in Philadelphia. Kathy could allow no consideration of mitigating circumstance to soften her stance or enable a middle ground of understanding and reconciliation. For a father to desert his motherless child and not write to him for thirty years was, she insisted, 'unnatural' and unforgivable and in that she remained steadfast to the last, her instinctive outrage still burning like a flame, even if the original sin of the father was by then more than a century downstream.

Kathy could clearly recall my grandfather visiting her one evening in 1931, when she was not long married and he himself had only a year left to live. He told her that he was emotionally upset: he had learned only that day that his father had died in America. I don't know how this news had finally reached Carrick, causing my grandfather to grieve that evening. Perhaps some returning emigrant told him something of it. The writer of the single letter seeking forgiveness had died unanswered sixteen years before. His son's evident distress on learning of that distant death tells its own story and evokes Pascal: *The heart has its reasons which reason knows nothing of.*

On my final day in Philadelphia I plant a tree to mark my pilgrimage. While Bernard and Grace drive to collect it from a nursery across the river in New Jersey I dig the planting-pit in their garden, in the place where the earlier freak storm had split the quince tree. It is the hottest day I've experienced. I am an Irishman digging and sweating in Philadelphia and earning blisters on his hands. Grace chooses a River Birch in memory of the boatman of Suir and Delaware. I water the roots and fill in the earth about them. Around the tree we drink a toast together. Parting with the Crokes is an affecting moment. They too have become entangled in the Oven Lane story since they called on us in Carrick on a day of teeming rain less than a year before and the gratitude I owe to them is beyond measure. When the time comes for us to leave our farewells signify something more final than we could know or want to know. This will prove to be the last time I will ever see Bernard Croke.

'Dave's Limo' takes us to New York where among the milling cosmopolitan multitudes at Kennedy Airport we are amazed to run into Carrick friends who happen to be travelling on the same flight back to Ireland: Tom and Pearl Nealon returning from a holiday, Paddy and Bobby Clancy on their way home from a singing tour. At a crossroads of the world the old local saying is dusted off and traded as conscious cliché: *Wherever you go you're sure to meet a Carrickman.*

Hours later in the sky I'm still awake when the first pastel-pink glimmer begins to seep up on the dark horizon. My wife sleeps beside me. This is a story of two rivers and two places an ocean apart; of two young mothers lost in childbirth; of a father and a son adrift on an estranging undertow of dislocation, poverty and pain, and of a poem searching out the silence of the story. In my luggage is a small sachet of earth from New Cathedral Cemetery which I mean to scatter on the grave at the Franciscan Friary in Carrickbeg. Out of the glimmering world high up between time zones my imagination shapes a symmetry of encounter. I fly eastward through the dawn to Ireland while on the ocean more than five miles below James Coady passes me in another dimension and direction, sailing westward to America in 1885. He looks up at the sky, wondering what lies ahead of him.

Good luck to them now, and safe may they land,
They are pushing their way to a far distant strand,
They are leaving their homes and facing away
For thousands are sailing to Amerikay.

There is much that I can never know and that the bare bones of the public record can never reveal. A dark pattern of human suffering and loss had sent and then pursued this man across an ocean. I can only guess at the day-to-day detail of James Coady's life in America, and am not disposed to moral judgement. I know nothing specific of his nights, his mornings, his sayings, his songs. My imagination lends him a face and travels with him through days and nights and years, into saloons and slums, churches and squares and avenues, into rooms, railway stations and trolley cars, through the bustle, babel and chaos of waterfront and warehouse. Can there be random undiscovered shards of public or private record still waiting to be found, or to find me? Was there a photograph taken in Philadelphia on the June day of 1886 on which he married Mary Brunnock of Ballinderry at St Malachy's?

Eternal greetings to the dead . . . Before this tale is told, Joe Shanahan, the basket weaver and sacristan, has crossed the river, and so has Kathy Coady, who remembered my grandfather's distress on learning of his father's death sixteen years on, and the old book collector Hugh Ryan who led me to Eileen McConnell. Gone too is Bernard Croke, who spoke and joked with me on the telephone from Philadelphia one day in August 1992, and died only minutes after we had said goodbye. We had been discussing arrangements for my participation in the Perceptions programme of the Irish American Cultural Institute following my trip to Philadelphia of the summer before. Under that programme in the following autumn I told my Oven Lane story to audiences in Chicago and Cleveland, Kansas and Cincinnati, Milwaukee and St Paul. At the end of that speaking tour I flew into Philadelphia to spend a few days with Grace, share her bereavement and visit Bernard's grave as well as those of my kin.

On our way to shop or post office I often walk along the quayside of the Suir with my children and turn up with them through Oven Lane to Main Street before we circle back to our house in the Poorhouse Field. Before our marriage my wife Martina worked above the lane in Bourke's Drapery, where Hugh Ryan the bookman also spent his working life, and where my grandfather Michael served his Victorian apprenticeship over a century ago. Once a year or so I am hauled into Bourke's for ritual refurbishment. I try on new clothes, among old ghosts.

The summer of 1990 brought the birth of our third child, a son. We named the infant Michael James for reconciliation and Marcus for remembrance of his mother's father. From the later migration by another James, a Coady in Connecticut made his christening shawl. The basket weaver made his crib.

Old Bridge and Weir, Carrick-on-Suir. *Do you remember this place*

Acknowledgements

Versions of some of the foregoing work first appeared in the following publications: *The Kilkenny Anthology* (ed. Macdara Woods); *Poetry Ireland Review* (eds. John Ennis, Máire Mhac a' tSaoi, Moya Cannon, Michael Longley); *Poetry*, Chicago (ed. Chris Agee); *Prize-Winning Radio Stories* (RTE/Mercier); *Riverine* (ed. Edward Power); *The Nationalist* (Clonmel) *Centenary Supplement* (ed. Brendan Long); *Éire-Ireland*, journal of the Irish American Cultural Institute (ed. Thomas Dillon Redshaw); *Nexus*, journal of The New England Historic Genealogical Society.

Foremost amongst those to whom my gratitude is due are Jean and Peter Fallon, for bringing to this publication the qualities of care and excellence that distinguish The Gallery Press. In respect of writing residencies I wish to thank Brendan Flynn, Clifden Community Arts, and also Pat Murphy and the Board of Kilkenny Arts Week. In general and particular ways I am indebted to Tomás Ó Nialláin, Mícheál Briody, Dick Denny, Barry Walsh, Joe Kenny, John Denby, Tony Fitzgerald, Jim Ballantyne, Máire Ní Chanainn, Edward Power, Proinsias Ó Drisceoil, Liam Hogan, Dick Meany, Tony Kehoe, Patsy Fitzgerald, Caitríona Clutterbuck, Jack Ryan, Eric Sweeney, John Ennis, Dudley Snidall and Siobhán and Seósamh Mac Ionmhain. I thank Séamus McGrath for the unfailing support and enrichment of his friendship over many years and remember also the constancy and goodness of the late Don Byard.

Within the context of 'The Use of Memory' I could not overstate my indebtedness to Eileen and Ken McConnell of Maryland and also to Grace Croke of Philadelphia and her late husband Bernard. I am thankful also to John McNamee, Robert McGovern, Joseph Meredith, Dennis Clark, Mick Moloney, Dr Eoin McKiernan and James Rogers. In the same connection I acknowledge the kindness of my hosts during an Irish American Cultural Institute speaking tour in 1992: Stan & Mary Hampl (St Paul); Joe McGovern, Mary Pat O'Connor (Chicago); Barney & Marge Heeney, Bob & Jeanne Dunn (Topeka); Barbara, Bud & Mary Kruser, Phil & Mary Joe Hanrahan (Milwaukee); Tom & Lonnie

McCauley (Cleveland); Tom & Eileen Ward (Elmhurst, Illinois); Jane Davoran, Eileen Conway, Dick & Mary O'Neill (Cincinnati).

In the spring of 1997 the author's arrangement for multiple voices of the poem 'All Souls' was given public readings at Butler House, Kilkenny, and Garter Lane Theatre, Waterford, by Moira and Róisín Clancy, Walter Dunphy, Roseanne Glascott and Tom Nealon (members of Brewery Lane Players, Carrick-on-Suir) along with the author and Harry Doherty, musician. A further performance on the occasion of the book's launch at Carrick-on-Suir Heritage Centre on 12 December 1997 included actress and director Peg Power.

The photograph on page 47 is by John Denby; the photographs on the cover, pages 8 (Cots on the River Suir), 11, 23 and 81 are by Michael Coady.